MESSAGE OF BIBLICAL SPIRITUALITY
Editorial Director: Carolyn Osiek, RSCJ

Volume 15

The Apocalypse

of

John

Seán P. Kealy, C.S.Sp.

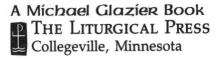
A Michael Glazier Book
THE LITURGICAL PRESS
Collegeville, Minnesota

ABOUT THE AUTHOR

Seán P. Kealy, C.S.Sp., is Rector of Holy Ghost Missionary College in Dublin. Previously, he served as a missionary for many years in Kenya, where he was also a professor of scripture at Kenyatta University. Among his publications is *Mark's Gospel: A History of Its Interpretation.*

A Michael Glazier Book published by The Liturgical Press

Cover design by Florence Bern

ISBN 0-8146-5581-5

TABLE OF CONTENTS

EDITOR'S PREFACE

One of the characteristics of church life today is a revived interest in spirituality. There is a growing list of resources in this area, yet the need for more is not exhausted. People are yearning for guidance in living an integrated life of faith in which belief, attitude, affections, prayer, and action form a cohesive unity which gives meaning to their lives.

The biblical tradition is a rich resource for the variety of ways in which people have heard God's call to live a life of faith and fidelity. In each of the biblical books we have a witness to the initiative of God in human history and to the attempts of people not so different from ourselves to respond to the revelation of God's love and care.

The fifteen volumes in the *Message of Biblical Spirituality* series aim to provide ready access to the treasury of biblical faith. Modern social science has made us aware of how the particular way in which one views reality conditions the ways in which one will interpret experience and life itself. Each volume in this series is an attempt to retell and interpret the biblical story from within the faith perspective that originally formed it. Each seeks to portray what it is like to see God, the world, and oneself from a particular point of view and to search for ways to respond faithfully to that vision. We who are citizens of our twentieth century world cannot be people of the ancient biblical world, but we can grow closer to their experience and their faith and thus closer to God, through the living Word of God which is the Bible.

The series includes an international group of authors representing England, Ireland, Canada, and the United States, but whose life experience has included first-hand knowledge of many other countries. All are proven scholars and committed believers whose faith is as important to them as their scholarship. Each acts as interpreter of one part of the biblical tradition in order to enable its spiritual vitality to be passed on to others. It is our hope that through their labor the reader will be able to enter more deeply into the life of faith, hope, and love through a fuller understanding of and appreciation for the biblical Word as handed down to us by God's faithful witnesses, the biblical authors themselves.

Carolyn Osiek, RSCJ
Associate Professor of New Testament Studies
Catholic Theological Union, Chicago

1

INTRODUCTION

The Apocalypse — A Modern Book

According to Edward Schillebeeckx (*Jesus*, p 144), whatever
one may think of apocalypticism, it is fundamentally an
existential, realistic, even a modern experience in this nuclear
age. For apocalypticism wrestles with the problem of cruelty,
pain, unhappiness, vengeance, discord, inequality, war and
injustice in the world, despite the belief that a good God is the
source of all life. It is the proclamation of the coming of a
radically new world, a Utopian yearning for a final end to
human suffering, a realization that God alone can establish a
kingdom of true peace, and therefore a radical question as to
the Church's role in the modern world.

Many are surprised to hear that Jesus of Nazareth lived his
life roughly in the midst of a period (from mid-second century
B.C. to the second century A.D.) when apocalypticism was
one of the most important influences in the religious thinking

of Judaism. With the publication in 1800 of 1 Enoch, the longest of the non-canonical apocalypses, the great discoveries in this field took off and continued until the Qumran discoveries placed apocalyptic firmly in the centre of the New Testament world. At the beginning of the twentieth century scholars such as J. Weiss and A. Schweitzer criticized the nineteenth century liberal understanding of Jesus and rediscovered the importance of the apocalyptic thinking of his time. Typical of the liberal approach were the writings of A. von Harnack (*The Essence of Christianity,* 1900). For Harnack the gospel was the great declaration of the spiritual liberation of humanity which was suffering in his day from a threefold threat — the state, the indifference of the masses, and the timidity of superifcial Christians. He was well aware of the apocalyptic sayings but interpreted them as merely "a manner of speaking," as high-pitched and highly coloured language not to be taken literally. Jesus used a contemporary manner of speaking in order to stress the vivid reality of the kingdom and God's decisive role in its coming. One could, therefore, dispose of the outer shell. The important part was the kernel which consisted of those aspects of his teaching in which Jesus differed from contemporary apocalyptic views and teaching. For Harnack the essence of the gospel contained three items: first, the present kingdom which enters the soul through Jesus' healing and forgiving; second, belief in the fatherhood of God and the infinite value of the soul rather than the nation; third, the higher righteousness and the commandment of love, as exemplified in the Beatitudes, the Good Samaritan parable and the golden rule.

Scholars such as Weiss and Schweitzer pointed out that apocalyptic expectations were prominent not only in the

kingdom sayings in the gospel but particularly in the Son of
Man sayings. They accused their predecessors of being
deliberately blind to these elements and of completely failing
to do justice to the whole gospel. They insisted that Jesus' view
of the kingdom was entirely an apocalyptic concept, totally in
the future, although he believed that the kingdom was
imminent. Like a prophet he had only spoken of it as present
so as to make vividly real both its imminence and his complete
assurance of its coming. Schweitzer concluded that Jesus
expected the world to come to an end during his own ministry
(Mt 10:25) or at least soon after his death (Mk 9:1). Another
modern scholar, John A.T. Robinson, the author of *Honest to
God*, also wrote a book, *Jesus and His Coming* (Abingdon, 1957),
in which he claimed that Jesus never taught a Second Coming;
rather all such references were creations of the early Church.
Texts such as Mark 8:38 and 14:62 (Dn 7:13) refer to Jesus'
going to the Father, not to his coming again.

Modern scholars tend to agree with variations of these two
schools of interpretation. The problem is that there is little or
no direct evidence that Jesus himself either encouraged or
expected an imminent vindication. Jesus was not "only an
apocalyptist" as some scholars have suggested. In contrast to
some apocalyptists who both preceded and followed him, he
seemed to have a remarkable reserve in his sayings. The
famous "pillar passage" in Mark 13:32 seems essential in any
reconstruction of his views. There he denies omniscience
about such matters as the parousia in a way which no early
Christian would have been likely to invent. Although Jesus
probably used some apocalyptic imagery, he seemed far more
preoccupied with the urgency of "today," with the
opportunities and challenges of the present situation.

Certainly Jesus' ministry was addressed to many who posed apocalyptic questions similar to our own, questions about suffering, about the meaning of a person's life, about the destiny of our world and universe, about ultimate justice, and about our profoundest hopes for liberation and lasting peace. According to Schweitzer, Jesus believed that his ministry would be the ending of history and the coming of the kingdom of which the contemporary apocalyptic writers dreamed, a kingdom of which he would be the leader. Almost all research in this century into the phenomenon of Jesus has been an attempt to respond to this understanding of Jesus.

Today the claim is made by some influential scholars that Christianity even began as an apocalyptic sect within ancient Judaism. Certainly the earliest days of the Christian Church were noteworthy for an intense degree of apocalyptic fervency. This arose especially when early Christians felt alienated from the structures of society, and has continued to encourage Christians ever since to hope for a new age particularly whenever the frustrations of the old seemed beyond repair. The dramatic statement of Ernst Käsemann in 1960 that Apocalyptic was:

> the mother of all Christian theology — since we cannot really class the preaching of Jesus as theology

provided a perspective for a re-examination of the New Testament and its contemporary literature. Käsemann suggested that the apocalyptic sayings do not actually come from Jesus himself but from the early Church, which, after the resurrection, became apocalyptic in its views and expectations. Thus Jesus' sayings about the kingdom were rephrased and adapted to the new views and situation. This was not done with any intention of deception but rather to draw out and make explicit what was already implicit in Jesus' sayings and career.

Especially today, apocalyptic writing is important because, amid the fear and chaos of the contemporary nuclear world threat, it provides a sense of meaning, purpose and direction to so many who are confused. The wide appeal of Hal Lindsey's book, *The Late Great Planet Earth* (Zondervan Publishing House, Grand Rapids, 1970), which, with an amazing 15 million copies in print, has been described as a major cultural force and one of the outstanding non-fiction best-sellers of our time, is a good illustration of the appeal of apocalyptic writing today. Lindsey treats academic biblical scholars with scorn and accepts literally such statements as 1 Thess 4:17:

> then we who are alive . . . shall be caught up together with them in the clouds to meet the Lord in the air . . .

Recognizing that today "the future" is big business, Lindsey notes, for example, that the French spend more than a billion dollars a year on clairvoyants, gypsies, faith healers, seers and prophets. Paris has one charlatan per 120 citizens, compared with one doctor for every 514 citizens and one priest for every 5,000. For Lindsey, the Bible clearly demonstrates that the judges, prophets, and kings, not to mention Jesus and the apostles, saw God at work in the historical events of their time. Similarly a confident pattern can be discerned in the events of our time particularly since the "prophetic countdown" began with the establishment of the State of Israel in 1948. This event supplied the key clue for Lindsey and led him to collect a set of predictions from such biblical books as Isaiah, Ezekiel, Daniel, parts of the synoptics, and Paul's letters and the Apocalypse. Three themes are spelled out: the Second Coming, the State of Israel, and God acting in history. However, a deeper analysis suggests that Lindsey's basic aim is to defend the American economic dream and way of life by a random use of convenient scripture texts and an appeal to the cosmic fear which is so pervasive.

Prophesying the end of the world is a common activity of Christian fundamentalist evangelical preachers. Until the 1970s they avoided political thinking and concentrated on saving "souls" from the slaughter of Armageddon. Then they increasingly began to give Biblical apocalypticism a contemporary political interpretation, envisaging the end as beginning with the "Rapture" or the rescue of all Christians to some place with Jesus "in the air" (2 Cor 12:3; 1 Thess 4:17). Those left behind will endure a period of tribulation for seven years. Then Russia and its allies, the evil northern empire of Ezekiel 38–39, will swoop down on Israel, which, in turn, will be helped by the seemingly benevolent leaders of the ten-nation European Common Market. A huge army of Chinese and Indians will come from the east and God will destroy Russia. But the European leaders will turn out to be Antichrist. They will enter the restored Temple in Jerusalem and demand veneration; Israel will refuse. Then Christ and his army of raptured saints will return to defeat the Antichrist in a battle at Armageddon, north of Jerusalem. After this, many Jews will accept Jesus as their saviour and a thousand years of peace will follow until the Last Judgement.

An interesting critique of the perversion of religion by those Christian fundamentalists who identify the nuclear holocaust with the Armageddon threatened by God in the Bible is to be found in Jonathan Schell's book, *The Fate of the Earth* (New York and London, 1982), one of the most discussed books in recent times. According to Schell, this identification arrogates to us not only God's knowledge but also his will, for it is not God who is threatening us but we ourselves. There is a great difference between God's Day of Judgement and the meaningless and completely unjust extinction of humanity by nuclear war. In the former, God not only destroys the world but also raises the dead to mete out perfect justice to all. To suggest that God is guiding us in the nuclear arms race is, according to Schell, the ultimate evasion of our responsibility as human beings, a responsibility based on the free will implanted in us by God.

Whatever one may think of popular books such as Lindsey's and their direct application of the Bible to the contemporary situation, it cannot be denied that they have sensed the mood of the times and challenge the Church to a deeper reflection on the meaning of the Apocalypse and its motifs of vindication, universalism, dualism and imminence. The fact is that we live in an age when apocalypse has tended to become a purely scientific phenomenon. For nearly five hundred years the scientific and technological revolution has proudly claimed to produce the seeds of future happiness for all, in contrast to the claims of our rather pessimistic religious heritage. Some perceptive scientists such as Whitehead have even suggested that the Christian interpretation of reality was closely associated with the rise of science. Now science is in a state of disarray. Far from its being salvific, many writers have even described it as hostile to genuine human progress. There is a growing recognition that because ultimately all questions are theological, science can never solve the spiritual problems of people. There are many indications that an uncritically accepted theology of pessimism and doom pervades the secular community. If Christianity has something to say, it will be through its own transcendent and wonderful version of the apocalypse, which is not total and absolute doom. Ultimately the apocalypse is a religious interpretation of the secular events of our time.

This recent fascination with apocalyptic, or lust for certitude, as it has been described, is in sharp contrast to the confident assertions of the demythologising school of Rudolf Bultmann. For Bultmann, to use electric light and other scientific advances, while still believing in the mythology of the New Testament, is contradictory. However, such statements can be seen as part of the avoidance which many scholars in contemporary culture have developed on the question of ultimate meaning and the mystery of the universe. Recent years have seen a radical reevaluation of mythmaking as an enduring function of human beings in every age. The development of science and history has not meant the end of mythmaking but the liberation of myth from science and history. It has led to the clarification of its power in illuminating the human condition and its role in helping people cope with the ultimate in life. The simple fact is that the journey of every society is held together by a myth system. This complex of thought-forms dominates all its activities, but it defies adequate intellectual formulation and lies beyond the field of empirical and scientific verification. Myth, far from being an objective assessment of the human situation, is a subtle, often indirect invitation to the whole person — imagination, feelings and behaviour — to live, to become involved, to commit oneself to certain values, to a certain pattern of life. In fact people are continuously engaged in mythmaking as they endeavour to relate to the mystery which is fundamental to the human condition. An important aim therefore of critical exegesis is to help people to re-mythologize themselves so as to tune into the mythological wavelength of the Bible. Many, who have been educated to believe that the only facts are scientific facts, need to pass through the critical phase, to recover the "narrative innocence" which permeates the biblical texts, to quote a phrase of Edward Schillebeeckx.

However, a modern person is normally a critical person and so has no hope of returning to the so-called primitive naiveté of the original biblical audience. To use the language of Paul Ricoeur, a modern person can relive the symbolic stories in a second naivete. This is achieved in and through criticism which examines the whole text and reflects on the evidence available. However, the ultimate purpose of true criticism, is not to destroy but to restore the power of the story, to loosen its bonds and to risk letting the sacred flow, through its retelling, into a modern encounter between God and the lived experience of the whole person. This contrasts with the common tendency to provide an exhaustive explanation of events with no room for the intervention or control of God. To read the Apocalypse from the point of view of Christian faith is to meet the person of the risen Jesus. Such an encounter, to quote the popular slogan, is dangerous to one's expectations, lifestyle, values, presuppositions and hopes. Contemporary interpretation of apocalyptic seeks to tread a middle path between the outmoded and somewhat naive application of Lindsey and the rejection of apocalyptic spirituality as mere wish fulfillment and projection as found in Frank

Kermode's provocative study, *The Sense of an Ending* (Oxford, 1966). For Kermode, even though the patterns of apocalyptic may persist, they are inevitably destined to end in tragedy and even absurdity. Likewise, in his famous *1984*, George Orwell predicted:

> If you want a picture of the future, imagine a boot stamping on the human face — forever.

Some of the best of modern theologians such as Karl Rahner (*Theological Investigations*, Vol 4, New York and London, 1966), Jürgen Moltmann (*The Theology of Hope*, New York, 1967) and Wolfhart Pannenberg (*Revelation as History*, London, 1969) have dedicated considerable energy to this task.

Controversy is nothing new to the Apocalypse. Since the early centuries of the Church it has continually wavered between being totally neglected and being the happy hunting ground of religious eccentrics who delighted in drawing from it detailed schedules of the last days. In fact, only with difficulty was it included in the official canon of the Church. Jerome articulated the basic problem, which so many have echoed ever since, when he described the Apocalypse's containing as many mysteries as words (Letters 53:9). The historian Eusebius was hesitant to include the Apocalypse in the canon. Origen and Justin accepted it while the great fourth century Cappadocian Fathers, Gregory of Nazianzus, Gregory of Nyssa and Basil did not. Dionysius of Alexandria (c. 250) maintained that it was not written by John the Evangelist. Aware that many of the brethren prized it highly, he did not reject it outright. But he was very concerned, as many have been since, because of the use made of its prophetic utterances by heretical millenarians. The early third century Roman presbyter, Gaius, attributed both John's Gospel and the Apocalypse to the Gnostic Cerinthus. This anti-gnostic stance of the early Church postponed its full acceptance especially in the Eastern Church where it was finally accepted in 691 at the Trullan Synod. There is no Greek commentary before the fifth or sixth century. Further, it is missing from most of the Greek manuscripts of the New Testament until the ninth and tenth centuries. However, in his Easter festival letter A.D. 367, Athanasius supported its inclusion in the canon and brought the official disputes about its sacred status to an end in the West.

Despite the failure of its supposed prediction that Jesus would return soon, the Apocalypse, then, was eventually accepted into the traditional canon of the Church. Nevertheless, the controversies which it engendered have been unceasing, so that it can be rightly described as the least understood and the most misinterpreted biblical book in history. The reformers were particularly antagonistic. In his preface to the New Testament A.D. 1522, Martin Luther described "the true kernel and marrow" of the New Testament in the following order of priority: John's Gospel and his first Epistle; St. Paul's Epistles, especially Romans, Galatians and Ephesians; and St. Peter's first Epistle. These are the books which show Christ. They teach all that is necessary and salvific to know. Even if one should never see or hear any other book they are sufficient.

Luther, although dominated by apocalyptic thinking and considering the final judgement to be imminent, rejected the Apocalypse. He considered it to be neither apostolic nor prophetic. For in it Christ is neither taught nor acknowledged and the inspiration of the Holy Spirit is not perceptible. He criticized the writer for giving images and visions found nowhere else in the Bible and for his nerve in adding promises and threats for those who kept or disobeyed his obscure and unintelligible words. Calvin, significantly, wrote a commentary on every book in the New Testament except the Apocalypse. For Zwingli, it did not savour of the mouth or mind of John and so he bluntly rejected it as "not a biblical book." Erasmus questioned the identity of the author of the Apocalypse and the Johannine literature.

Similar criticisms are heard in the twentieth century. According to A.F. Loisy the best which can be said about the Apocalypse is that for centuries people have taxed their ingenuities to discover in it meaning which is not there. The simple reason is that the meaning, which is there, was immediately contradicted by the course of events. The philosopher, A.N. Whitehead, has faulted the Apocalypse for its barbaric influence on religious sentiment. For D.H. Lawrence, whose last work was significantly entitled *Apocalypse*, it typifies and reinforces the malicious attacks on the delights and achievements of human civilization by the envious have-nots of every age. He finds so much destruction in the Apocalypse that "It ceases to be fun." Nevertheless, Lawrence was very much attracted by the apocalyptic style of writing. A person's mind should likewise be allowed to move in cycles, to flit here and there over a cluster of images. This enables one to put aside the egotistical mentality, to realise that one is a small part of a vast whole. Of such a mind was the spirit which built the great cathedrals of Europe.

Even among influential biblical scholars one finds those who denigrate the apocalyptic. Adolf Julicher, who was famous for his rejection of allegory in favour of parable, made the famous judgement that "Apocalyptic is prophecy turned senile." Rudolf Bultmann, the great New Testament scholar of

this century, described it as "weakly Christianized Judaism."
The significance of Christ is merely to provide a certainty
which the Jewish apocalypses did not have.

For C.H. Dodd, the excessive emphasis on the future
effectively relegates to a secondary place the distinctive elements of Christianity —faith that, in the completed work of
Christ, God has already acted for the salvation of humankind
and the blessed sense of living here and now in the divine
presence. Despite the magnificence of its imagery and its
splendid visions of God's majesty and the world to come,
Dodd concluded that the conception of God's character and
attitude towards people falls not only far below Jesus' teaching
but also below the best parts of the Old Testament. Jesus' new
authoritative teaching about the infinite loving-kindness of
the heavenly Father is scarcely echoed except in a verse or
two. The fierce Messiah whose warriors ride in blood up to
their horses' bridles is quite different from the gospel portrait
of the one who went about doing good and healing all who
were oppressed by the devil. John's seven burning torches
together with the Eternal and the Lamb constitute an eccen-
tric and rather unorthodox Trinity. They are similar to the
Amesha Spentas of Zoroastrianism and are a product of
muddled fantasy thinking in sharp contrast to the notably
sober and rational doctrine of the Spirit found in the Fourth
Gospel.

But there has always been another side to the picture.
People of every generation have loved the Apocalypse. Not
surprisingly perhaps, Marxist ideologists including F. Engels
value the Apocalypse as the oldest and most significant Christian document because of its attitudes towards war and force.
But it is surely significant that artists, musicians, hymn writers
and folksong writers, poets and painters, and tapestry and

manuscript illuminators have been particularly attracted to
the Apocalypse and through it have influenced the spirituality
of preachers and believers for nearly 1,900 years, e.g., the
anonymous Song of Mary, "Hierusalem, my happy home"
and the popular Victorian song, "The Holy City". Even a brief
survey will illustrate the remarkable power of this ancient
writing to inspire some of the most sublime creations of the
human spirit making it, verse by verse, probably the most
thoroughly illustrated book in the Bible.

The visions in the Apocalypse of Christ in Majesty and the
Adoration of the Lamb adorn the triumphal arches of the great
Roman basilicas such as St. Mary Major (432-440). The fifth
century mosaic at St. Paul-Outside-the-Walls depicts the
adoration of the Lamb by the Twenty-Four Elders and the
Lamb enthroned between the seven Spirits of God (Apoc 4:5).
We are so accustomed to the idea that the crucifixion is the
supreme symbol of Christianity, that it comes as a shock to
realise that in early Christian art it hardly appeared. Few
crucifixion scenes before the tenth century make any attempt
to touch our emotions. The imagery of the Apocalypse was
dominant in the great churches of Europe, from the Twenty-
Four Elders who occupy the famous Rose Window of Chartres
Cathedral, to the Four Horsemen on the Last Judgement
portals of the cathedrals of Paris and Amiens, to the ninety
scenes of the Apocalypse in the immense east window of York
Minster. Unique, perhaps, among all these, is the collection of
seventy tapestries from the fourteenth century which are
found in the Castle of Angers in western France. This monu-
mental cycle included 98 scenes and 800 square meters when
intact. From modern times one could mention the huge
mosaic behind the altar of the National Shrine of the Immacu-

late Conception in Washington which depicts John's vision of
Jesus exalted in majesty.

   Famous artists such as Cimabue, Botticelli, Michelangelo
(*The Last Judgement* in the Sistine Chapel), Titian, El Greco,
and Holman Hunt (*The Light of the World*) have been strongly
influenced by the Apocalypse. The frightening and often
earthy paintings and woodcuts of Pieter Brueghel and
Albrecht Dürer have endeavoured to capture its imagery in
vivid details. Poets such as Dante and Milton, Yeats ("The
Second Coming"), devotional writers such as Bernard of
Cluny ("Jerusalem the Golden"), musicians such as Brahms
and Handel ("The Hallelujah Chorus"), and filmmakers from
Bergman (*The Seventh Seal*) to Coppola (*Apocalypse Now*), have
made the Apocalypse live on unforgettably. The visionary
John has been described by different writers as a creative
genius (Moffat Commentary) with a better sense of the right
word than a Stevenson, a greater command of unearthly
supernatural loveliness than a Coleridge, a richer sense of
melody and rhythm and composition than Bach, the only
masterpiece of pure art in the New Testament whose fullness
and richness and harmonic variety place it far above Greek
tragedy (Philip Carrington). John Ruskin was moved to tears
of penitence and joy. William Blake went into raptures over it.
Coleridge found in it the quintessence of symbolism.

   Once a book like the Apocalypse has been committed to
writing and launched into human history it becomes like
Tennyson's *Ulysses*, "a part of all that I have met." All
literature possesses an openness to potential meaning. As the
literary critics say, a text is no longer an object in itself but
reader-dependent for its meaning. It becomes a continuous
creative event interacting with its different readers, in their

unique situations, making their distinctive contributions. Each person will hear an artistic work such as a Mozart symphony differently. To one it will appear joyful, to another sad. A profound work such as the Apocalypse compels its readers to examine themselves, their theological stance and historical situation. If the person is a black African the nuances of the response will be different from those of a white African. One who is in prison will answer differently from a university scholar. A woman will see aspects which are denied a man. The variations are endless.

Reading the Apocalypse Today

The following pages are offered as a help towards a deeper reading of this unique biblical book for our time. They are written in the belief that at the heart of culture lies religion —the way in which people attempt to give meaning to the ultimate realities and to the values by which they live. The foregoing examples have amply demonstrated that apocalyptic spirituality has been at all times a key strand in the attempts of both Christians and non-Christians to relate not only to the time process in which they are intimately involved but especially to relate to the crisis of the world which seems ever new and to be particularly weighing upon the Western world today. The following thoughts are intended to be provocative because a person's spirituality is not a package deal which another can easily provide. Rather it is a search for quality in living, for values, for ultimates, for growth in hope. Each must make this journey for oneself. First the entire book should be read at one sitting of about an hour to get the total impression.

Reading aloud is recommended because this was the way the original audience heard the book. To write down one's first impressions and problems and compare them with later impressions is also a very useful exercise. Our first chapter suggests some approaches to reading the book. The next chapter is intended to provide a deeper appreciation of the unusual kind of literature involved, the modern attitude towards the Apocalypse presupposed, and the terminology and principles involved in the commentary. The main part, the commentary, consists of reflections based on the writer's reading of a wide selection of contemporary material on the Apocalypse. They aim at drawing out its spiritual meaning. A concluding chapter discusses in more detail some of the ways the Apocalypse has been seen through the ages.

Pascal in his *Pensées* criticized those authors who speak of "my book," "my commentary," because books contain more contributions from other people than from themselves. The discerning will recognize my indebtedness on every page. But a particular mention should be made of Sr. Tina Heeran M.S.H.R. and also of my friends Fr. Frank Soughley C.S.Sp. and Fr. Brendan McConvery C.Ss.R. who so often saved me from infelicities and obscurities.

A famous biblical scholar, Hermann Gunkel, once commented: "Bin ich zu ende beginne ich," ("When I am at the end I am at the beginning"). When the dust of scholarly wrestling with the text is over, a further reading at one sitting is recommended; and then, of course, the problem is to live in the spirit of the Apocalypse.

2

SOME WAYS OF APPROACH

Reading the Apocalypse or listening to it read aloud as it was originally intended to be experienced is to engage in a dialogue between the words of the author and the holistic response of the listener. Not only is the Apocalypse a unique work of art but its significance is unique for each person each time he listens to it. To adapt the ancient wisdom of Heracleitus: "You cannot step into the same river twice" because the river has already changed by the time one has entered it. A work becomes a classic because of its capacity to continually surprise. Further, the nuances of my response will be different if I am black or white, a man or a woman, in prison or free, in a minority or a majority, in a university or a more manual job, if I am a Christian, an agnostic or an atheist. For the Apocalypse is a kind of looking glass which at first sight seems to reveal its own author and his remote world. But in the end it reveals the reader as it probes his responses to the profound themes of the human condition of politics and religion, of life and death, love, hatred and vengeance, friendship, time and fidelity, the quality of our God and the presence of evil, and above all the meaning and quality of our lives. It especially questions the disturbing extent to which the consciousness of the Christian communities in the West has become assimilated to the structures and materialistic values of a so-called Christian or even post-Christian society.

Recent Views

The Apocalypse, with its invitation to go into the desert to take a hard look at the values, the gaudiness and oppressiveness, and the dehumanizing and anti-God atmosphere of our society, will lead some to very radical views. The author is not afraid of controversy or even exile and death. He bluntly condemns the views even of members of his own Christian community who seemingly compromised on such issues as eating meat which had been offered in sacrifice to idols. He insists like the Bible of old that his community should be a contrast society, a holy people with a social order different from that of other nations (Dt 7:6ff; Lv 20:26; Tit 3:3–6).

After reading the Apocalypse one can readily sympathise with the words of Oscar Romero, the martyred Archbishop of El Salvador:

> It is practically illegal to be an authentic Christian in our environment ... precisely because the world which surrounds us is founded radically on an established disorder before which the mere proclamation of the Gospel is subversive. (*The Tablet*, Dec. 1983, p 1251).

Nevertheless one must always remember that the Apocalypse reflects the situation of a very small community without political power, authority or armies, faced with the seemingly invincible power of the Roman Empire. The Church from Constantine's time onwards was in quite a different position. Nevertheless, the Church needs the blunt voice of the Apocalypse within its canon. But to see it as attempting to provide uniform, clearcut, theological options for every age would easily lead to such extreme criticism as that of John L. McKenzie (*The New Testament Without Illusion*, p 239):

> Apocalypse is the cry of the helpless, who are borne passively by events which they cannot influence, much less control. The cry of the helpless is often vindictive, expressing impotent rage at reality. Apocalyptic rage is a flight from reality, a plea to God that he will fulfill their wishes and prove them right and the other wrong. Apocalyptic believers could hardly think the saying, "Go make disciples of all nations" was addressed to them. Had apocalyptic believers dominated the church since the first century, there would have been no missions to unbelievers, no schools, no hospitals, no orphanages, no almsgiving. The helpless cannot afford to think of such enterprises, they can only await the act of God and then complain because that act is so long delayed. The Gospels and the Epistles rather tell the believers that they are the act of God.

More positively, theologian David Tracy (*The Analogical Imagination*, p 265f) insists that apocalyptic thinking has a central corrective role which challenges all present Christian interpretations. It functions as a challenge:

to any purely "private" understanding of the Christian event by forcing a recognition of the genuinely public, the political and historical characters of all Christian self-understanding; as a challenge to all the privileged to remember the privileged status of the oppressed, the poor, the suffering in the scriptures; as a challenge to all the living not to forget the true hope disclosed in these texts of a future from God for all the dead; as a challenge to all wisdom and all principles of order to remember the pathos of active suffering untransformable by all thought ordering cosmos and ethos; as a challenge to each to remember all; as a challenge to face the reality of the really new, the "novum" and the future breaking in and confronting every present, exploding every complacency; as a challenge of the sheer intensity of the "pain of the negative" in the cross needed as an intrinsic moment in any adequate theology of incarnation or any present oriented theology of resurrection; as a challenge to remember the eschatological "not-yet" in every incarna-tional "always-already" and even every "but-even-now" resurrectional transformation; in sum apocalyptic may be viewed as a major context and a signal key to the intensification principle itself in all New Testament expressions.

So far we have indicated, however briefly, three modern thought-provoking reactions which help us reflect on the importance and relevance of the Apocalypse for our times. A fourth reflection can be drawn from the application of Aristotle's theory of catharsis in Greek tragedy by Adela Yarbro Collins in her interesting study entitled *Crisis and Catharsis*. She endeavours to explain the effect which the Apocalypse had on its first readers and how it achieved its effect in helping them overcome the unbearable tension between the reality of their lives and what ought to have been in the light of the resurrection of Jesus. The writer's aim was to create that tension for those unaware of it, to heighten it for those who felt it already and to help both overcome it in an act of literary imagination. Aristotle's medical word "catharsis" referred to the removal of alien, painful matter from the body, restoring it to its normal state. Through the experience of tragic plays he believed that our often vague and inarticulate emotions of fear and pity were aroused, intensified and given objective expression. The result was not their complete removal but rather that their painful and disturbing aspects were purified and removed to some extent. The Apocalypse deals with such emotions as fear of the Roman authority and resentment of its wealth and power which are evoked and intensified by John for his audience. The forces which threaten are symbolised by the beast from the abyss and the dragon, projected, clarified and magnified onto an exaggerated cosmic screen. Likewise in chapters 17 and 18 with its description of the gaudy prostitute, its list of luxury items which were unattainable for his audience, resentment is provoked. But the repeated accounts of the destruction of their enemies and their city produces a catharsis and a feeling of control. Thus the writer cleverly deals with the feelings of powerlessness or aggression, and the thought and attitudes of his audience by his use of affective symbols, by drawing them into his narrative, and by continually keeping them in suspense about the outcome because they recognize that their own destiny is intimately connected with the conclusion.

Nonetheless, a clear recognition of the limitations of the Apocalypse seems essential. In particular it contains no specific program for meeting the challenges posed by the realities of John's day or the similar realities of our own. However, in A. Collins' view (p 174) the Apocalypse "supports the current trend in which the churches take public stands on social issues, a trend that is well established in the mainline Protestant churches, reviving in evangelical and fundamentalist circles and now spreading to the Roman Catholic Church."

The Modern Crisis of the Imagination

To turn to the Apocalypse from the rest of the New Testament is like entering a strange foreign land full of angels, trumpets and earthquakes, strange beasts, dragons and a bottomless abyss. Reading it for the first time with only a limited acquaintance from hearsay is like the experience of Mark Twain described in *The Innocents Abroad*. Carried away by the exotic sights of oriental Morocco in 1867, he exclaimed: "The pictures used seem exaggerated — they seemed too weird and fanciful for reality. But behold they were not wild enough. They have not told half the story."

Perhaps much of our difficulty in hearing the Apocalypse comes from our lack of appreciation of the role of the imagination, of the value of imaginative power in the service of religion. To a large extent we are children of the Enlightenment with its enthronement of reason or rather its combination of scepticism, empiricism and rationalism. In our search for wisdom to help us with our problems we tend to turn to the scientist, the sociologist and the engineer rather than the poet or the visionary. We are suspicious of the imaginative, the emotional, the passionate, the subjective in favour of the factual, the down to earth, the precise, the verifiable, the objective. Archibald MacLeish has put it quite well (*Listen to Love*, p 208):

> The Crisis of our time as we are beginning slowly and
>   painfully to perceive is not a crisis of the hands but of the hearts.
> The failure is a failure to desire.
> It is because we the people do not wish-
>   because we the people do not know
>   what it is that we should know
>   what kind of world we should imagine
>   that this trouble haunts us.
> The failure is a failure of the spirit;
>   a failure of the spirit to imagine
>   a failure of the spirit to imagine and desire.

Certainly, on both these criteria of imagination and desire John scores highly in contrast to modern theologians who have consistently underplayed the role of the imagination. The latter have tended to stress the intellect, the reason, the idea, although the imagination should be understood with Wordsworth, as reason in her most exalted mood, or with Newman, as the creative power of the intellect. With the breakdown of the great medieval synthesis exemplified by Dante, Thomas Aquinas, and the great cathedrals of Europe, what T.S. Eliot described as "dissociation of sensibility" in theology, literature and art took place. Feelings and emotion were abandoned to poetry while mind and ideas were the basis of science and theology. Truth was identified with clarity. Not many years ago, one learned theologian, who was well versed in the Greek Fathers, probably the most imaginative school in church history, expressed scepticism at the idea that the imagination could make a contribution to theology (cf Brian Ahearne C.S.Sp., *African Ecclesiastical Review*, 1984, pp 32ff). But recent scholars have begun to highlight the disastrous consequences of this absence in the contemporary Church.

For Patrick W. Collins (*More Than Meets the Eye*, pp 7ff) what is missing in the contemporary liturgical renewal is "Mystery," the experience of the holy. What was present prior to our inadequate renewal with its overemphasis on clear understanding and easy participation was imagination. This is the part of our knowing powers which enabled a writer like John to help his community to experience mystery and communion. The various forms of imagination, such as image, symbol, myth and ritual, help to transform our vision and our values, to reorientate our own most basic moods, feelings, reactions and actions, our way of living on this planet. God's truth is disclosed more fully through the imagination than through logic and abstract concepts, words and notions. Imagination helps us to get more deeply into existence, into the really real world, to see people including ourselves in a new and more whole way. Its language, by addressing the imaginative system, engages the whole person, leading, not merely to a notional assent of the mind, but to a real assent, a continuing religious conversion and commitment. As Cardinal Newman once put it, faith begins not in the notion or concept but in the image or symbol. Therefore, he insisted that for our assent to be rationally adequate "it must be first credible to the imagination." We can all distinguish with Gerard Manley Hopkins between

> an equation in theology, and dull algebra of the schoolmen, or knowledge that leaves . . . minds surging, poised on the quiver . . . the ecstasy of interest (Collins, pp 34f).

One of the best known homilists of recent years, Walter J. Burghardt S.J., once argued that four problems prevent today's homily from being any improvement on yesterdays' sermons: fear of Sacred Scripture, ignorance of contemporary theology, unawareness of liturgical prayer, and lack of proper preparation. Gradually, he realised that what he described had a lamentable omission (*Sir, We Would Like to See Jesus,* p 5). A homily which is only a masterpiece of Cartesian clarity lacks something vital and lifegiving. He had left out the most serious aspect of all, the imagination, the creative power or capacity to make the material an image of the spiritual. This capacity he found in Rembrandt's self-portraits, in Beethoven's Fifth Symphony, in the perfume of a new rose or the flavour of old wine, in storytellers like C.S. Lewis and J.R.R. Tolkien, in dramatists like Aeschylus and Shakespeare, in poets from Sappho to e.e. cummings. No wonder the great scientist Albert Einstein could insist that imagination is more important than knowledge.

Key Themes

GOD

No other biblical book paints such a majestic and cosmic picture of God, lord of all history and master of the ultimate destiny of all his creatures. While painting the majesty of God in unforgettable scenes, John, like a poet, is especially sensitive to the rejection of God in his world, to the pervasive smell of evil, the presence of rebellion, violence and tragedy, the deep seated desire for revenge. Yet he does not lapse into dualism.

Only one God is lord over all and he allows evil its limited course to run (13:5ff; 17:17).

Like a heavenly oriental monarch, God's most characteristic title is "pantokrator," an expression which literally signifies one who is in total command of everything (in the universe). This term which John repeats eight times is found only once more in the New Testament and that in an Old Testament quotation (2 Cor 6:18). John opposes the god of the seemingly all-powerful Roman emperor and defiantly cries out his battle hymn, his invitation to rejoice: "Alleluia, The Lord is king, our God the Almighty" (19:6).

But this God is not a remote God. Rather, he is a paradoxical mixture of anger, justice and caring. He is Exodus God who is, and was, and is to come (1:4). He can enter into a gentle relationship with his suffering people to wipe away every tear, even death itself, from their lives, and to make them into a kingly and priestly people who will serve him joyfully in his new creation. God's history is not a chaotic jumble of events but has a purpose and a destiny. As few New Testament books do, the Apocalypse asks the blunt question of the seemingly helpless Christian community: On whose side do you stand? Yet there remains a further question: Can anything be done about the seemingly hopeless situation of the world? John's answer is the Lamb, an image which he repeats 28 times in his book. As he begins his seven-seal vision he insists that no one else can open the book of history, to realize its meaning and to accomplish God's purposes.

CHRIST

What is clearly distinctive about John's Apocalypse in comparison to contemporary Jewish Apocalypses is the fact that it is Christ-centered from beginning to end. The whole work insists that Jesus Christ is the faithful witness, the first-born of the dead (1:5), a divine being who shares the throne of the almighty God himself. In the new creation there is no temple because the Lord God and the Lamb are the temple (21:22ff). It is difficult to distinguish the titles applied to Jesus from those attributed to God himself. Christ is the Alpha and Omega, the first and the last, the beginning and the end (1:11;22:13). He holds the keys of Death and Hades (1:18). He is Lord of Lords and King of Kings (17:14). He is the lion of Judah and the root of David (5:5;22:16). But the lion is above all the Lamb who triumphs and shows the way to triumph through self-sacrifice. John's book uses the words victor, victory and vanquish more often that the rest of the New Testament combined as it leads into the most detailed description of the final triumph of Christ in the New Testament.

But it is precisely the idea of the triumph of Christ presented often in lurid apocalyptic imagery which presents so many problems to western commentators with their ideals of serenity or at best stoic apathy. To live in a world without a passion for justice would be to turn human existence, in Macbeth's words, into a senseless tale told by an idiot. An element of severity and vengeance is essential to any love worthy of the name. To concentrate only on the gentler aspects of love is a serious distortion. Great literature from Homer onwards shows that a deeply felt and rationally guided anger is healthy and even necessary for coping with our circumstances. Yet there is no encouragement in the Apocalypse of crusades or holy wars of any kind, only to faithful witness. It is not difficult to see how E.F. Scott's view of John's Christ is a total exaggeration when he points out that he has

> nothing to say about love, humility, forgiveness. He frankly hates his enemies and rejoiced in their downfall. In the whole course of the book we can catch hardly a distant echo of the Sermon on the Mount ... From the Revelation it could never have been gathered that Jesus was compassionate, that he healed the sick and encouraged the helpless and outcast and bore our infirmities, that he was meek and lowly of heart ... As we know him from this book Christ is a great but terrible figure, righteous but implacable, the champion of his people, but breathing destruction on his enemies.

This rather superficial view recalls the description of the German H.J. Holtzmann, who saw John's Christ as a murdering Messiah taken over from Judaism and one who celebrated his triumphs in glaring contradiction to the peaceful Messiah-concept of Jesus. John is not writing a Christian gospel and cannot be condemned for what he is not trying to do. Rather, he presupposes a Christian community well-instructed in the Christian gospel. Apart from the martyrdom mentioned in 2:13, the communities to whom he is writing do not live in a situation of persecution. But they obviously are small communities faced with seemingly insurmountable odds from an empire to whose allurements it would be all too easy to succumb. The essential message of Jesus is the comforting "Fear not" of the gospels (1:17). Jesus shows an intimate knowledge and concern for each of the communities. The picture of Christ criticising, reproving and inviting the communities to return to love is close to that of the synoptic Jesus: "Whoever is dear to me I reprove and chastise . . . Here I stand knocking at the door, if . . ." (3:19f).

The invitation of John is to look beyond the present state of suffering and seeming triumphs of evil, and to anticipate sharing in the joy of the marriage supper of the Lamb (19:7ff). It is an invitation to praise, to Hallelujah. If it had nothing else, the seven great songs of praise would have made this book worthwhile. One can make a case for the idea that John expects all to be saved, that all creation will in the end sing the praises of the Lamb (5:9-13). Certainly God's will is that the good news is proclaimed to everyone (14:6). John's goal is a universal Christian community dialoguing with its risen Lord, listening to his words of purification and drawn to answer the invitation of the Spirit and the Bride with their commmand "Come" — to answer in like manner by echoing the Christian creed "Jesus is Lord," saying "Come, Lord Jesus" (22:20).

THE HOLY SPIRIT

Statistically speaking the Holy Spirit does not figure as prominently here as one might expect. Yet on examination the scope of John's treatment is quite adequate although rather different from the other New Testament writers. John does not use the term "Holy Spirit" but often uses "spirits" in the plural. Although he uses the phrase "the spirit," his meaning is not as clear as that of the other New Testament writers. John does not seem to distinguish whether an inspiriation or revelation comes from the spirit, the Son of Man, the angel(s), or "a loud voice." Particularly in the main part of his book they come from angels who are like commentators interpreting what is happening.

A good place to grasp John's reflection on the role of the Spirit is to recall how he considers himself a prophet and how he describes his book as prophecy. John reflects the use of Ezekiel in contrast to the classical prophets from the eighth century onwards for whom the spirit is not expressly the source of inspiration. Ezekiel however uses visions and ecstasies as media of the spirit's activity. Four times John attributes his great heavenly visions of ultimate reality to the spirit: twice "I became a spirit" (1:10; 4:2) and twice "the angel carried me away in spirit" (17:3; 21:10).

But for John, the Spirit, which is like a sevenfold flame continually burning before the throne of God, is not just the bearer of visions (1:4; 4:5). Above all the Spirit who is sent into the whole world (5:6) is the one who brings the presence and especially the words of the risen Christ. In each of the letters to the seven churches the audience is exhorted to listen to the message of Christ which is conveyed by the Spirit (2:7). Furthermore, the role of the Spirit as confirming and giving further understanding of God's promise is found in 14:13 where "The Spirit added, 'Yes, they shall find rest from their labours, for their good works accompany them.'" Finally, the spirit inspires the Church by speaking in the hearts of the believers the words which sum up its hope:" Come, Lord Jesus" (22:20).

THE CHURCH

John's book can still speak to us because it was addressed originally to real flesh and blood communities of Asia Minor struggling, succeeding and often failing to live the ideals of the Christian life. His picture of the early Church is a welcome warning against the temptations of Christians of every age to idealise the early Church, its survival and its success in passing on the Christian message. The seven letters, symbols of the universal Church and its response, show how aware John is of the variety of responses which people make to the Gospel in every age. Ephesus had orthodoxy and patient endurance but was in danger of discouragement and its charity was waning. In wealthy Smyrna the Christians were materially poor though spiritually rich. They had suffered trials with more to come. Pergamum had held fast in the face of attacks from outside but had been careless with false teaching within the community. Thyatira was commended for its "agape," its faith and service but criticised for its tolerance of a false prophetess. The Church at Sardis was spiritually asleep and in fact dead despite its contrary reputation. Philadelphia had little power but stood fast in trials. The affluent Church of Laodicea was really poor, blind and naked. This critique keeps the Apocalypse tied to our real world.

Christianity, for John, is a moral religion in which there were always Christians who failed. His book has well been described as a sustained piece of hortatory moral teaching using the apocalyptic literary form. He roundly condemns idolatry, theft, uncleanness and untruth while praising patient endurance, faithful and zealous witness, chastity and love. This human dimension so typical of the Bible keeps the book from any kind of triumphalism. Yet he also insists that the Church consists of these real people who are loved by Christ and who have been redeemed by his blood, to become a royal priestly people (1:5ff). Although convinced that history has a meaning and a purpose and that the Church has a glorious future, John holds out no prospect for peace and justice on earth before God's triumph. Until then life will be a constant struggle with the two beasts, the instruments of Satan. Persecution and martyrdom (witness) are key aspects of the Christian life. Jesus himself is the exemplar, the faithful witness (1:5). His faithful followers, though small in number, provide the only real opposition to the beast and his many worshippers. But even they too need to be washed in the blood of the Lamb (7:14; 12:11).

There is a continuous tendency among commentators to measure the martyrs and their desire for justice against the morality of the Sermon on the Mount with its unique command "Love your enemies," as if this were the central teaching of the New Testament repeated in every book. Certainly the Apocalypse falls short of this ideal and is corrected by being placed in the New Testament canon to interact with the other New Testament books. However it is being increasingly recognized that each book of the Bible is by itself an inadequate representation of the full gospel of Jesus. The many different witnesses of the twenty-seven book canon are required for this. To put too much emphasis on the distinctive witness of any book runs the risk even of heresy. Books like the Apocalypse, with its aim to strengthen people in their witness to Jesus in the face of the seemingly invincible empire, naturally use the black and white techniques of caricature. However, the danger is to criticize John on the basis of the contemporary, rather superficial and sentimental concept of love of neighbour or the empty niceties of modern diplomatic language. The uncomfortable fact in the Bible is that, apart from the rare statements of Jesus in Matthew and Luke about love of enemies, whenever there is mention of interpersonal love in the New Testament it is a question of love within the Christian community of faith, of the brethren for each other. This love is admittedly open-ended. But there is no naive emphasis on all people being actual brothers and sisters. The Apocalypse is in keeping with the rest of the Johannine literature in its lack of emphasis on the love of enemies as a theme. However, both have in common the view that God's loving care is directed towards the salvation of the whole world community particularly in the suffering of the Lamb. Both agree that the mission of the Christian is to testify to the reality of that incredible love in our world such as it is. The gospel must be preached to everyone without exception.

POLITICS

As Charles Péguy once said that everything begins in mysticism and ends up in politics. Because of the contemporary emphasis on the struggle to maintain the integrity of the gospel in the midst of political ambiguity and the limitations of the structures of our society stressed by liberation theologians, there is an understandable fascination with the radical, political anti-Roman position which John encouraged his audience to take. Quite likely John himself was one of those wandering charismatic leaders who imitated the wandering of the Lord himself (Mt 8:20; Lk 18:29f). Their function was to appeal to the conscience of the different communities which they encountered and to pose in stark terms and in the name of the risen Lord a radical challenge to many of the comfortable values of ordinary life, from family values, to wealth, to political life. The world will always need such people to point to the beastly characteristics of the whore of Babylon, because Babylon is present in every age, particularly our own. It symbolizes that falsely independent human spirit seen in the builders of the city and Tower of Babel, in Nineveh and Tyre and Rome and in a thousand other arrogant empires which oppress people in every age. Although one must confess that they had no alternative programme to offer apart from moral exhortation, it would be the opposite extreme to dismiss such views as too simplistic, too narrow and too harshly judgemental.

The Bible is not confined to one political image or model. Contemporary research has disclosed in it at least six different political models including theocratic, neutral, prophetic, the migrating nation, the new world and liberation. Any attempt to apply the Bible to modern times must take into account this wide spectrum. Each however has its limitations. But all agree in seeing political action essentially in terms of religion and theological reflection.

One can consider John a prophetic critic of society. But the prophets in Judaism are basically conservatives who have little or no interest in creating new structures for a more humane society. They were satisfied with the law and structures as they found them. A particular refinement of the prophetic view, developed by the apocalyptic writers, is the eschatological model to which the concluding chapters of the Apocalypse bear witness. This model envisions the transformation of the present imperfect world into a new heaven and a new earth (Is 2:2ff; 11:2ff). There is however only a superficial similarity to the Marxist and secularist hope for a revolution to be built on supposedly historic and scientific considerations which are quite different from the prophetic expectations in the Bible. The latter are based on God's direct intervention, not on our achievement. Left to ourselves, the human story will stutter on with its obvious imperfections and continually oscillate between its temporary triumphs and its frequent disasters.

John does indeed use holy war imagery to interpret his world and the ultimate resolution of its conflicts between good and evil. But ultimately there is no final battle, just the all powerful decrees of God and his victorious Lamb. Faithful passive resistance even unto death where necessary is what is advocated for the Christian community, but not recourse to the violent approach of the Zealots. The little attention which the Bible seems to give to many of what we consider vital issues is constantly disconcerting. The point was well made in the incisive comment attributed to the great scholar, Rudolf Bultmann: In a time characterised by great social inequalities Jesus only once in a parable seems to refer to the situation.

HOPE

The hope of Judaism is not limited to a purely future expectation of a higher life transforming suffering and death. Neither does it ignore our present world and its problems. Rather it is a combination of both future and present being transformed. However much John may have borrowed from Jewish apocalyptic theology, his work is free of superficial irrelevant speculations. Thoroughly dominated by the risen Christ, he is concerned with giving hope to his Christian communities in their present situation. Their lives have meaning and will have a worthy conclusion. In contrast to Judaism, for the Christian the decisive eschatological event has already taken place in the life and particularly the death of Jesus. The final age has begun. There is a direct relationship between their decision for Christ and his kingdom — surrounded though they are by the seemingly invincible and attractive kingdom of Babylon — and their final destiny.

A superficial reading may suggest that for John this world is of little consequence. But reflection shows that he is deeply concerned with the blasphemies and injustices of this world to which the new creation is "coming down." Evil need not have the last word in our lives. His message is that love is possible, even essential, here and now because God has first loved us. In this atmosphere of God's love he invites his community to sing a new song, a joyful Hallelujah, despite the problems of society.

Above all, John's Apocalypse is an invitation to a vision of hope beyond the tragedies and seeming pervasiveness of evil in our world. As the Vandals and Gothic hordes converged on Rome, Augustine, from his pulpit at Hippo (Sermon 105), gave an unforgettable expression to that hope of John in words which we roughly paraphrase as a fitting conclusion to our reflections:

> Listen carefully to the gospel, you miserable people who imagine that the world is about to be destroyed: "Though heaven and earth will pass away, my words will stand." Enough of your weeping and wailing. Are you not yourselves responsible for this fate which is overwhelming you? People are saying: "These are difficult times." But are not these times part of ourselves? They are what we have made them to be! Yes, we are all guilty, but we have been promised mercy. Have you not all been baptized in hope? Do you not understand that God's will can be accomplished through the most frightful affliction. No Goth can seize what belongs to Christ. True riches are not things which vandals can steal. No barbarian can rob you of true life.

3

LOCATING THE APOCALYPSE IN ITS OWN WORLD

Literary Form

Whoever wishes to make the Apocalypse relevant to our times must first accept the basic fact that it was originally written to criticize, to encourage, and to give hope and a sense of mission to Christian communities in late first century Asia Minor. The common title or indication of its literary type as Apocalypse can, in fact, easily lead to misunderstanding and misinterpretation. On closer examination the literary form turns out to be a hybrid type bringing together the literary forms of letter, prophecy, liturgy and apocalyptic. The author describes his work as an apocalypse in the opening verse. More frequently he speaks of it as a prophecy (1:3; 10:11; 19:10; 22:18–19), but in fact he presents it as a letter to the seven churches. Therefore, instead of being a work of purely apocalyptic propaganda or a mere product of the contemporary revival of apocalypticism in Asia Minor, it should be seen as a critique of contemporary apocalyptic expectations and speculations similar to the second letter to the Thessalonians. John does not interpret Jesus and his teaching in the light of apocalyptic but rather the reverse. He rereads apocalyptic in the light of Jesus.

Like Paul, the writer uses a letter format, particularly in 1:4—3:22. This has the effect of solidly grounding the apocalyptic flights of the centre of the book in the concrete experiences, hopes and failures of the Christian community in Asia Minor. The writer himself describes his work as a prophetic message (1:3), thus situating himself within the long line of Jewish prophets. These were the unpopular critics who ceaselessly warned against the tyranny of absolutizing the institutions of the "status quo" and who fearlessly endeavoured to call the Jewish leaders and people back to their covenant faith and commitment. The great achievement of the prophets, who for long periods existed as a minority report in Israel, was that they enabled the Jewish people to survive the collapse of all their human institutions, to find some meaning in the disasters which they were experiencing. Faced with the imperial designs of Egypt, Assyria, Babylon, Persia, Syria, and Rome, they managed to maintain a sense of identity and to survive disasters which wiped out almost all of their neighbours. The fact is that Jewish apocalyptic owes a considerable amount to the Old Testament prophets. Some recent scholars such as P.D. Hanson (*The Dawn of Apocalyptic*, 1975) conclude that apocalyptic results from a long process of development which goes back even to pre-exilic times. This is particularly true of eschatology. Critics like Gerhard Von Rad who find some characteristics of wisdom literature in apocalyptic, however, cannot fit eschatology into their view that the wisdom tradition was the mother of apocalyptic because in the extant wisdom literature there is no concern with eschatology. Already in Ezekiel 38–39,   Zechariah 9–14 and parts of Joel there are apocalyptic tendencies. But the transition to apocalyptic can clearly be seen in Isaiah 24–27,   four chapters joined later to the work of the great prophet. These chapters contain such apocalyptic themes as the universal judgement, the eschatological banquet, and signs in the heavens. However, the first and most important book which merits the title Apocalyptic is that of Daniel. Daniel was anonymously written in the climate of persecution, terror and death which marked the oppressive rule over Palestine of Antiochus 4th, called Epiphanes (175–164 B.C.). The atmosphere is quite similar to that which John's work emphasises.

Apocalyptic and Prophecy

Nevertheless, although they share much in common, apocalyptic literature is to be carefully distinguished from prophetic. Both see the Exodus Yahweh as the Lord guiding all history. Both foretell the future though not in a detailed way as if they had special information unknown to others. Both have visions of judgement and hope. Both are mainly concerned with repentance and with exhortations to faithfulness. The prophets, before writing their oracles, met their audiences in a face-to-face encounter with the direct words of Yahweh himself. The hearers were accused and threatened with punishment and disaster if they did not repent of their injustices before it was too late. The prophet had a certain limited confidence in the institutions of society and a hope that, at least in theory or with God's help, society could be changed for the better.

John's work, at least in the opening letters, shares this view. But normally apocalyptic was a written work directed towards the faithful to offer them encouragement while judgement and punishment were reserved for their oppressors who were considered to be God's enemies. The prophets had a strong future dimension to their preaching such as Amos' Day of Yahweh, Hosea and Jeremiah's new Exodus, Isaiah and Micah's just king, new Zion and peaceful kingdom or Jeremiah's new covenant. However their aim was to change their hearers and present to society what it should be. By contrast there is little or no hope for a present change in the apocalyptic writers. The present time is so much under the control of evil that a catastrophic intervention of Yahweh himself is needed to produce the New Age. Apocalyptic proclaims that an understanding of the present and the future is not to be found in the priests and their interpretation of the Mosaic Torah or in the wisdom tradition with its search for a rational understanding achieved by human effort alone. The mystery of God's guidance of history towards its end is to be found only when God chooses to reveal it. For John, the authoritative interpretation of the present suffering comes from the risen Jesus whose martyrdom began the final period of history. An obvious characteristic of apocalyptic is its esoteric nature and its delight in symbols (numbers, names, fantastic beasts, angels, demons) and visions, grotesque figures and cosmic upheavals such as no surrealist or Kafkaesque artist ever dreamed of. These enabled John to give a disguised but authoritative review of world history, such as we find in Daniel. The aim was not to give new information but to give assurance of lasting victory to the faithful, to point out that the time of persecution, turbulence and warfare was the darkest hour before the dawn.

The problem with the word apocalyptic is that like eschatology it has become a rather ambiguous term which embraces a rather wide range of different meanings. The outstanding example of the apocalyptic type in the Old Testament is Daniel. But Daniel is not exactly typical of the other examples found in Jewish literature outside the Bible. If one were to reduce them all to a common denominator, that would mean little more than a religious interpretation of history, a concern for the future salvation of the whole world and the use of visions and vivid imagery to express that concern. Certainly John's work is not a typical apocalypse. These books were normally written using the pseudonym of one of the ancient heroes such as Enoch, Ezra, and Daniel. But John's work is not pseudonymous. Like the prophets to whom he is closer than to his contemporary Jewish apocalyptic writers, he speaks in his own name as a witness to the living God. His vantage point is not of a figure of the past who surveys history up to the present and predicts the future, but of a person well known to his contemporaries for whom he writes as their fellow sufferer (1:1,4,9; 22:8). He not only identifies himself and the circumstances in which he received his revelation but also describes the situation of his audience. His central emphasis on Jesus as the slain lamb, returned to life (1:18; 5:6,12) and present in the community, radically distinguishes John's Apocalypse from similar Jewish writings. Neither does he place its visions in a fictitious place. Here one can see a sharp contrast to the approach of the writer of 1 Enoch 1:2:

> Enoch . . . saw the vision of the Holy One in the heavens,
> which the angels showed me, from them I heard everything,
> and from them I understood as I saw, but not for this genera-
> tion, but for a remote one which is to come.

The letter form gives the whole a personal and pastoral touch concerned with the real historical situation of the churches of the time. The visions of heavenly realities are directly related to earthly events. His book is not a visualized book in the normal sense of the term vision. Rather it is an artificial intellectual one, as anyone who has struggled with his seven-headed and ten-horned monsters will testify. His vision is essentially a careful mosaic interpretation of scripture, particularly Ezekiel and Zechariah, in the light of his belief in the presence of the risen Lord. However, even though the visions are to some extent literary devices, this does not deny the possibility that they are basically rooted in some visionary experiences of the writer. His heaven is not so much a second story to the world but rather the background, the all-embracing Lordship of Jesus in which the world stands. While he invites his audience into an extra-ordinary world of the imagination, yet he is a realist of the fantastic, to use a phrase once written by Joseph Conrad about H.G. Wells.

Interpretations

John is careful to regularly provide both explicit and implicit interpretations of many of his images. This probably implies that the rest were familiar to his audience or could be guessed rather easily by them. He gives at least ten deliberate interpretations throughout his book in 1:8,13; 8:3; 10:1ff; 11:7; 13:6,18; 14:14ff; 17:9ff; 18:21; 19:11ff. Implicit interpretations are found in such texts as 4:1–11; 5:6; 6:1–8,12–17; 12:1. In a recent article (*Interpretation*, January 1984, p 41), David L. Barr sensibly points out that we must keep our heads in the midst of the exotic symbolism of the Apocalypse and remember that they refer to quite common everyday prosaic realities. Stars are the churches (1:20); eating books is prophesying (10:9–11); an angel with a golden censer before God's throne, suddenly throwing it on earth with thunder, lightning and earthquake ensuing, is one of John's lively liturgical celebrations (8:3–5); the gaudy prostitute riding on a scarlet beast is the provincial John's view of the grandeur of late first century Rome. Some of his symbols involve surprising transformations. The conquering lion of Judah is the Lamb (ch 5). The conquest of the dragon by Michael and his angels in heaven is in reality achieved by the suffering of the Lamb (2:11). In the climactic scene, where the victor on the white horse arrives to make war on the beast, the victory is gained by the word of Jesus and the word about Jesus (19:11–21). It is not only Jesus' death but also the witness of his faithful followers which slay the wicked. Thus John reinterprets the traditional apocalyptic motifs to portray in story form his belief that faithful witness leads to judgement and salvation. But if John merely spoke of the prosaic realities, his work would have been robbed of its imaginative power and the intellectual and psychological response which he hoped to evoke.

His pastoral advice is solidly based on the assertion of the present reality of the kingdom with the assurance that this Jesus will come "soon" (1:1,7; 6:11; 11:15; 22:6–20). The whole has a thoroughly Christian dimension which is particularly evident in the place it gives to Jesus as the meaning and end of all human history. Irrelevant speculation and other flights of fancy are avoided.

Author

There is no good reason to deny the statements of the Apocalypse that it was written by John on the Aegean island of Patmos (1:4,9; 22:8). However, because of differences in language and terminology in theological argumentation and concepts, scarcely any critical scholar today atributes the Apocalypse to the same author(s) who wrote John's gospel and 1,2,3 John. Nevertheless the fact is that, early on, all five works were included under the aegis of John the Apostle. However, there are similarities between the content (Christ and his salvation, spirit, angels, satan, church, eschatology, sacraments) and form (duality, metaphors, numerical symbols, groupings, Old Testament citations) in the Apocalypse and the other Johannine writings which cannot be attributed to a common Jewish background. The famous remark of the third century bishop of Alexandria, Dionysius, that "it scarcely, so to speak, has a syllable in common with them" is a gross overstatement. Dionysius, who was anxious to combat the spread of literal millennial teaching in his diocese and to disassociate it from the evangelist John, noted that there were many Christians named John in Asia. Curiously in contrast to the Gospel and Epistles, the author of the Apocalypse names himself. Dionysius also pointed out that the rather good style of the Gospel and Epistle contrasted with the inaccurate

Greek usage and barbarous idioms of the Apocalypse. A number of scholars explain John's violations of the accepted rules of Greek syntax by supposing that because he was better acquainted with Hebrew or Aramaic than Greek, he would naturally lapse into non-Greek expressions quite frequently. Another possibility is that the use of his peculiar Semitic Greek is a kind of protest against the sophisticated Hellenistic culture which was so prevalent.

Although most modern critics agree with Dionysius, the striking parallels between the Gospel and Apocalypse should be noted. In only these two works in the New Testament Jesus is called the Word of God, admittedly with a different emphasis in each. A key concept for the Messiah in both is the Lamb-allusion to Isaiah's poem (Is 53) although the Greek words are different. Zechariah's "pierced Messiah" is found in John 19:37 and Apocalypse 1:7. Other aspects in common are the importance of witness and giving testimony, the spiritual interpretation of terms such as life and death, hunger and thirst, and to conquer. However, the emphasis of the Fourth Gospel on realized eschatology contrasts so sharply with the intense expectation of final salvation in the Apocalypse that one cannot imagine that the same author wrote both works to the same audience at the same time.

The unknown John is content to describe himself as brother (1:9) and prophet (22:9). He probably was a wandering prophet who had worked for a time in each of the seven communities which he mentions (1:4). In 18:20 and 21:14 he mentions the Twelve as if he were not a member. He seems to have a close knowledge of the situation in Asia Minor and presupposes that his readers knew him well. The fact that he is exiled at Patmos "because I proclaimed God's word and bore witness to Jesus" (1:9) shows that he was a Christian missionary whose activity led to his exile. His thorough knowledge of Judaism has led many to conclude that not only was he a Jew but also that he was born in Palestine. Nevertheless, he was no Judaizer for he does not insist on the Sabbath, circumcision or the cultic regulations of the Law and his condemnation of idolatry and the eating of meat sacrificed to idols suggest some knowledge of the problems discussed in Acts 15.

Date

A first reading suggests that either the author has a psychotic imagination, or that he wrote during a time of intense persecution from the Roman government (2:13; 3:10; 6:9–11; 14:12f; 17:6). At least he seems to have *expected* an intense period of persecution to break out very soon. Such texts as 6:9f; 16:6; 17:6; 18:20,24 and 20:4 presuppose that the blood of apostles, prophets and many other Christians had saturated the streets of Rome and cried aloud for vengeance. During the first century after Christ there were only two periods when Christians experienced such direct antagonism from the Roman emperor and government: the second half of the reign of Nero (54–68) and the final years of Domitian (81–96). Nero's persecution seems to have been limited to the city of Rome. He did not conduct the kind of systematic persecution throughout the empire which John seem to presuppose. Neither did he try to compel Christians to worship him as a god.

The situation which more credibly fits the Apocalypse is that of Domitian. A very negative and paranoiac portrayal of

Domitian is given by such ancient writers as Pliny the Younger, Tacitus, Suetonius and Juvenal. They say that Domitian even demanded to be worshipped as Lord and God (Dominus et Deus). Yet there is no evidence of a formal decree compelling this veneration throughout the empire. Some recent scholars have suggested that the negative portrayal of Domitian was due to the desire of these writers to flatter Trajan and the benefits which he conferred. The writers of Domitian's own court do not address him as "our Lord and God." The people who suffered in Domitian's persecution were probably sympathisers with Judaism, and it is by no means certain that any were Christians. The simple fact is that the Christians did not share the privileged exemptions of the Jews. Any refusal to take part in civic and religious honours to the emperor would have serious social, political and economic consequences. Local Roman officials could demand the acknowledgement of the Roman gods; and therefore persecution, torture, banishment and even death were an ever present liability. John is probably referring to some local persecution in Asia Minor. He may have exaggerated his portrayal of persecution to strengthen his communities in their response to the imperial cult and to the dangers which many quite likely were ignoring. Certainly his letters to the seven communities such as the wealthy church at Laodicea show no indication of widespread persecution.

John's book is unique in the New Testament in being dated in the early tradition. Irenaeus, himself a native of Asia Minor who claims to have known Polycarp who knew John, expresses the almost unanimous tradition. Writing with regard to the name of the beast (13:18) he says that the Apocalypse "was seen no such long time ago, but almost in our own generation, at the end of the reign of Domitian" (c. A.D. 95). No convincing alternative has hitherto been proposed. However, Domitian never engaged in a worldwide persecution of Christians and popular descriptions of it seem probably to be exaggerated by later writers. At Rome even members of the imperial family were executed in his Christian persecution. But Asia Minor seems to have become a centre of the imperial cult and to have suffered persecution. In the nineteenth century a broad consensus of scholars favoured a date at the end of the sixties — Nero died in 68 and Jerusalem fell in 70. But in the twentieth century the consensus favours a date in the persecution of Domitian. Probably the best solution to the problem is to admit that part of the text originally referred to the Neronian persecution and that the final author used it to strengthen his community in their present persecution. The fact that we do not have definitive answers to the historical and critical problems is not as great a loss as might be imagined at first sight. In fact the theology of this book can be adequately studied apart from such questions.

Place

The text shows the influence of John's place of exile, the isle of Patmos, which is located in the Aegean Sea between Greece and Turkey, about 37 miles west to southwest of Miletus or 50 miles to the southwest of Ephesus. Some 16 square miles, it is about ten miles in length and six miles at its greatest width. It had a mild climate. Pliny the Elder's description of Patmos as a place of banishment makes it easy to understand why in the new earth "the sea was no longer" (21:1). The apocryphal

Acts of John describes several miracles worked there. In the eleventh century an influential monastery was founded on a mountaintop in the middle of the island. A grotto in the hillside with a magnificent view of the sea is pointed out to visitors as the place where the visions of the Apocalypse took place. Significantly, the word "sea" is used no less than twenty-five times, making the Apocalypse full of "the sights and the sounds of the sea." The rising and setting of the sun turn Patmos into a wonderful "sea of glass mixed with fire" (4:6; 15:2).

Outline

There are nearly as many outlines of the book as there are interpreters of it. Different attempts to rearrange and even improve the present text have been offered. A brief survey of recent commentaries shows that there is no perfect solution. However, from the beginning of the twentieth century greater precision in literary analysis has been achieved. In keeping with the more recent tendency, the approach adopted here is to interpret the text as we have it.

It is relatively easy to distinguish the prologue (1:1–3) and the epilogue (22:6–21). The prologue is followed by a general introduction giving greetings and the story of the vision (1:4–20) and then by a series of seven letters criticising even churches in Asia Minor (2:1—3:22). However, the subdivision of the remainder does not lead to any certain conclusions. The development of the thought is not linear. Given the nature of the book as one of vision and ecstasy, one must accept a certain amount of incoherence, of what has been

described as untamed disorder. Chapters 4 and 5 can be seen
as a more particular introduction presenting the main characters, God, the Heavenly Court, the Lamb, and the Book of
Seven Seals. The following structure is offered as a help
towards reading the text and no more.

A.	1:1 3	Prologue
B.	1:4–20	Introduction to Vision on Patmos.
C.	2:1–3:22	Seven Letters to a very Human Church.
D.	4:1–16:21	The "in-between" time of the Church.
	1) 4:1–5:14	An Introductory Vision of the Court of Heaven.
	2) 6:1–7:17	The Opening of the Six Seals.
	3) 8:1–11:15	The Seventh Seal and the Sounding of the Seven Trumpets.
	4) 12:1–14:20	The Vision of the Woman, the Dragon and the Two Beasts.
	5) 15:1–16:21	The Seven Last Plagues.
E.	17:1–18:24	The Verdict on the Great Harlot.
F.	19:1–10	Alleluia — Victory — the Lamb's Wedding.
G.	19:11–20:15	The Coming of Christ and the Final Victory.
H.	21:1–22:5	The New Creation.
I.	22:6–21	Epilogue: Concluding words to the reader from Patmos.

4

COMMENTARY

A. *Prologue — An Invitation to Happiness, 1:1–3*

John, in his opening verses, describes his work as an invitation to blessedness, to happiness. He is careful to describe five links in his chain of communication: God, Jesus, his angel, his servant John, and the servants to whom he is writing. The work he is writing is not his own product for he is only a servant. "Servant" is that popular Old Testament word used frequently in the New Testament as a title of honour to describe the special representative of Jesus.

Even a brief reflection on the earliest Christian document (1 Thess 1:10) shows that his service is simply to present the apostolic preaching in a different kind of literature

> to await from heaven the Son he raised from the dead, Jesus who delivers us from the wrath to come.

In such Pauline texts as 2 Thes 1:3–12; 1 Cor 2:6–8; 2 Cor
4:4,17; Rom 8:18; Eph 6:11–18, we find the opposition to the
true God instigated by the devil and demonic forces, a two age
dualism and the idea that present sufferings will yield to future
glory in the eschatological judgement. This will bring punishment to the opposition and comfort to the afflicted. Paul, in
dealing with his communities' problems, has no difficulty in
using curses and threats, ironic and sarcastic rebukes, but also
reminders of blessings.

We can describe his work as a reflection on the Beatitudes
— "Blessed are the poor . . . those who are persecuted . . . ."
The theme of God's blessing runs right through the Bible,
from the special blessing spoken personally by God to the
newly created people in Genesis to the restoration of the
blessing of all people through Abraham and especially through
his descendant Jesus. Perhaps the originality of Jesus can be
seen more clearly in his Beatitudes, his prescriptions for
happiness, than in any other sayings. The provocative statement of Francis Bacon that, while prosperity is the blessing of
the Old Testament adversity is the blessing of the New, is a
convenient summary of the newness of Jesus' approach and
his radical demands. In his classical book, *Israel*, J. Pedersen
once attempted to describe the meaning of blessing in the
Jewish tradition. Blessing is a vital power, it is the inner
strength of the soul filling it with the happiness it creates. The
soul is a whole which is saturated with power. This power
makes the soul grow and prosper so that it can maintain itself
as God's image and act as God's representative in the world.

John has seven beatitudes spread throughout his book. The
first one, given here in his introduction, is repeated twice for
emphasis at the end in 22:7 and 14. It pronounces a blessing

on the one who reads the words of his prophecy in the liturgical assembly and on those who hear and obey "because the 'kairos' is near." The other indications of happiness are death in the Lord (14:13), watchfulness on the pilgrimage through life (16:15), the invitation to the Lamb's wedding feast (19:9), and a share in the first resurrection (20:6).

The technical Greek term "apocalypse," which in Latin is translated as "revelation," is carefully explained as "the words of the prophecy." John's purpose, like that of the prophets of old, is not to provide new information to his Christian audience, for they are already familiar with the story and teaching of Jesus and the early Christians. His aim, like that of the critical prophetic conscience, is to recall what his audience already knows about Christ and, with the aid of the Jewish apocalyptic imagery, to deepen their understanding of what they already believed about the risen Jesus. His opening phrases such as the angel mediating between the divine (Jesus Christ and God) and the human (John and the other servants of God), the things which must take place soon, are typical of the Jewish apocalyptic tradition. Anyone who has attempted to visualise the seven-headed and ten-horned monsters, the dragons and horseman and other symbols, will quickly realize that a literary vision based on a reading of such books as Daniel, Ezekiel and Zechariah is what is involved in the vision of the seer of Patmos to which he bears witness.

A note of urgency is clearly struck with such phrases as "what must happen very soon" and "for the 'kairos' is near." But this emphasis on imminence never becomes a clear prediction — the future is in God's hands alone. Like the Qumran Essenes, the early Christians, as writers like Paul and Luke clearly show, were convinced that they lived in the expected age of the Spirit. They eagerly looked forward to the future coming of Jesus and were confident of the final triumph of God's guidance of history. They believed these attitudes were a continuation of the sense of urgency which character- ised Jesus' own teaching and ministry and in particular his interpretation of the Father's will. Eight further uses of the word "must" (4:1; 10:11; 11:5; 13:10; 17:10; 20:3,6) show that the author like Luke in particular sees God's irresistible plan of salvation at work in the world. This divine necessity does not lead him into any fatalism or denial of freedom to the people involved in his story or to any speculative answer to the problems involved. Rather, like the writers of the Old Testament, he is content to affirm the total sovereignty of Yahweh as Lord of history while insisting on the freedom and responsibility of the human characters involved, whether they be Christians, Jews, or Romans. The key to his vision is his view of God — his revelation has come ultimately from God who gave it to Jesus who in turn entrusted it to an angel who in turn shared it with John. But this God is no cruel, vindictive Babylonian type of God but one who is Father (1:6; 2:28; 3:5,21; 14:1) with all the intimacy and care which that caritative term suggests. The writer is convinced that the will of this caring God will ultimately prevail. In W.S. Gilbert's opera, *Princess Ida*, Lady Blanche, whose dreams and ambitions have not yet been fulfilled, sings defiantly words that express the spirit of the Apocalypse:

> Come, mighty Must!
> Inevitable Shall!
> In thee I trust.
> Time weaves my coronal!

Go, mocking Is!
Go, disappointing Was!
Away! The Mighty Must
Shall be!

B. Introduction to the Vision on Patmos, 1:4–20

Like Paul, John opens his letter with a densely worded theological greeting. Thus, like the prologue to John's gospel, he sets his basic theme and some of the topics to be treated in his critique of the seven churches in the western part of what we call Asia Minor. These were obviously not the only churches in the area (Ac 20:5ff; Col 1:2; 4:13) but they were probably familiar to the writer. They are all found on the circular road constructed by the Romans in Asia Minor. Beginning with Ephesus and passing through the other six churches, one would end up again at Ephesus. Since the author is so interested in symbolism, the use of seven, the number of totality, perfection and completeness, may suggest the wider audience of the church catholic.

The greeting "grace and peace" recalls the old priestly blessing of "covenant favour" (Gk "charis") and "peace" (Gk "eirene") found in Num 6:24-26. The Greek word "charis" signified that which gives delight or pleasure, the beauty, charm and attractiveness of a person or a movement. It was used to translate the common Old Testament phrase "find favour ("chen") with God." In Christianity it was used to express the heart of the good news, the free favour of an "abba" God to undeserving people, that wonderful quality of kindness towards sinners, of concern for the least, the last, and the lost, which animated the ministry of Jesus on earth.

In classical Greek "eirene" usually meant freedom from strife or war. But the Hebrew "shalom" had a much wider and richer meaning. It described according to one scholar, "a completeness, a success, a maturity, a situation which is both prosperous and secure withal, a state of well-being which is the direct result of the beneficent Presence of God." The word symbolizes the hope of Israel's prophets that, beyond their evident failure, God will grant a new covenant and bring about a deeper obedience among his people. For Isaiah, only justice will bring about peace (Is 32:17). In the New Testament, peace has come to signify the reconciliation between God and people accomplished in and through the saving life of Jesus.

The source of our grace and peace is threefold: God, the seven spirits before the throne, and Jesus. This description can best be taken as an elaborate triadic formula for the Trinity. The simple yet profound combination of the three tenses—is, was and is to come — for God is a paraphrase for the Hebrew tetragrammaton YHWH (Ex 3:14; Is 41:4) found only in the Apocalypse in the Bible. (It is also found in a Palestinian translation, Targum of Deut 32:39.) In verse 8, which parallels this verse, are added the first and last letters of the Greek alphabet and the words Lord God and the Almighty ("pantokrator," "the one who controls everything"). These images provide an emphatic picture of the total and absolute power of God in creation and over all history as a basis for John's later exposition of the present difficult times. The name of Yahweh which is more accurately rendered "I will be what I will be" implies a powerful sense of presence, an activity or a process accomplishing itself, rather than a mere statement of existence. A good case can be made for the claim that the motif of the presence of God provides a more unifying and dynamic principle and centre not only for the Old Testament but for the New Testament literature as well.

But Yahweh, above all, means a God who liberates the oppressed because of the concrete association of this name with the event of the Exodus. The Hebrew idea of God contrasts sharply with the basic Greek view. According to the Greeks, action is a sign of imperfection and the more perfect one is the less one acts. The Jewish view of God was of an active, involved God, for life expresses itself in action. God's activity was seen above all in the all-powerful act of creation and in the liberating activity of the Exodus. Thus in his opening words, our writer lays the basis by emphasising the tremendous power of a caring God who gets involved in the lives of people from beginning to end.

The reference to the seven spirits before his throne is to the Holy Spirit in his fulness — the word spirit is not used for angels in the Apocalypse — or perhaps to the activity of the spirit in the seven churches. The aim is to provide encouragement by alluding to the awesome power which was attributed to the Holy Spirit (Zech 4:6). The Spirit guided each church and each person who listened (2:7).

There are three references to Jesus' identity ("the faithful witness, the first born from the dead, the ruler of the kings of the earth") and three descriptions of his salvific activity ("loves us, freed us from our sins by his blood, and made us a kingdom, priests to his God and Father").

The word used for witness is "martyr." John, pointing out that Jesus was faithful unto death, is encouraging his community not to seek death but to be faithful even if it means death. The idea of faithfulness is very prominent in John's gospel (Jn 18:37). For Bultmann Jesus' witness is "to make

God's reality effective over against the world in the great trial between God and the world." The title "first born from the dead" is found in a hymn celebrating God's rule in Colossians (1:18), a letter where Laodicea, one of the seven churches, is mentioned. This emphasis on the resurrection gives further encouragement to faithful witnesses. The third title "ruler," connects the verse with Psalm 89:27 which was a messianic psalm in the rabbinic tradition. Psalm 89 is a national lament by the reigning king of Judah after a great military defeat. Since the king's Father is the God of the whole world, he has the right to claim world dominion over the rulers of the world, a claim also found in the other kingdoms of the ancient Orient. His only hope is that the Lord will be with him to strike down his adversaries and give him worldwide dominion. This hope is now realised in Jesus. Even though earthly kings seem to have their way, the reality is that it is Jesus who actually rules over the world. The theme of the kingship of Christ is a key theme for our writer (6:15; 11:15; 17:2,15; 19:16).

This reflection on the power and dignity of Jesus leads naturally to the first of many doxologies and to an eager description of the actual coming of Jesus at the end. These brief hymns of praise and expectation show the truth of the statement that true theology is born in celebration. The final victory is already being celebrated by the Christian here and now. Hymns of praise are found throughout the entire history of Israel. Their acclaim "To him who loves us" recalls the answer of the famous Swiss theologian Karl Barth when asked to summarize the theology of his large tomes. He quoted the Sunday-school song "Jesus loves me, this I know, for the Bible tells me so." The theme of love may not be numerically dominant in the Apocalypse (the verb is found elsewhere only in 3:9 and 12:11; the noun in 2:4,19; and the adjective in 20:9). Yet its use here in the present tense in a crucial introductory passage in which past, present and future are typically brought together is significant. The belief that Jesus' loving acceptance of death achieved our salvation parallels that of Paul and John's gospel. The Old Testament sacrificial imagery is in the background with blood standing as a symbol of life (Lv 17:11). We are free because of Jesus' death, free to become "a kingdom, priests unto God and his Father."

The kingdom was the central teaching of Jesus. Jesus himself was the kingdom, the activity of the liberating Father himself — as elsewhere in the gospels, even in the context of the kingdom, God is described by the intimate word, Father. Now those who have been loosed from their sins by the initiative of Jesus are somewhat surprisingly described as the kingdom. Some older translations changed "kingdom" into "kings" to make it parallel with "priests." The New English Bible uses "royal house." Jesus has raised Christians to the dignity of the royal family. A similar idea is found in Paul's statement that Christians have been give adopted sonship within God's family. This text, which has an important Old Testament background, teaches the doctrine of the royal dignity and priesthood of all believers. The Old Testament phrase "kingdom of priests" which is also echoed in 1 Pet 2:9 seems to mean that Israel was chosen as a people to give Yahweh true worship, but not that all Israel was empowered to offer cultic sacrifices. Only Yahweh is king while Israel is essentially a worshipping community. In the New Testament the idea is that Christians are a nation set apart and called to offer to the Father the spiritual sacrifice of a holy way of life.

But nowhere in the New Testament is there any reference to the priesthood of the faithful in the context of the sacraments or in liturgical worship. Nevertheless, the problem with an ordained ministry has led to the minimising of the appreciation of the priestly dignity of all the faithful. The fundamental sacrament of baptism which makes one a child of God deals with salvation. Therefore one's baptismal day is more important than any ordination day to a special ministry within the general priesthood.

The doxology concludes with the desire that to Jesus be given "glory and power" and ends with the customary Hebrew affirmation, Amen ("truly," "it is true"). The word "power" was currently used for political power. The use suggests that real power is and should be found with Jesus alone. The Apocalypse is a critique of the use of political power in every age.

The doxology naturally leads to (v 7) a dramatic prediction of the return of Christ ("Look, he is coming !") and a brief description of the events associated with it, a theme of crucial importance to his readers and to our generation. Writing a report from Rome during Vatican II, the French theologian Yves Congar commented:

> We are latecomers, and the only thing left (of the Creed) for us to corrode is belief in eternal life and the resurrection of the body. Atheistic communism and material technology, which is not a monopoly of Russia, has made this its special work and offers a religion of earthly security and comfort that has no need of belief in another life.

Verse 7 is a good example of the use of the Old Testament in the Apocalypse. It is not a direct quotation, but rather the whole verse had an Old Testament flavour (cf Mt 24:30; Jn 19:37). Although clouds are often associated with the coming of God (Ex 19:16), the reference here seems to be to Daniel 7:13 where a mysterious one like a son of man comes with the clouds of heaven, an expectation common in the gospels (Mk 13:26; Mt 24:30; Lk 21;27). The second part reflects the obscure prediction of Zech 12:10–14. The heavenly coming will be visible to every eye, even of those who pierced him —perhaps such people as Pilate, Annas, Caiaphas and the soldiers were still alive when John was writing. All the inhabitants of the earth will lament him bitterly in repentance or perhaps at the judgement which he brings. A double affirmation by the writer, "truly amen," concludes the quotation. Then the almighty God himself vouches for the certainty of the coming of Christ.

John then quickly gives own name and describes his solidarity with the suffering of his readers and his own call and inspiration to write a book to them.

An interesting parallel to this inspiration to write is found in the life of Dr. Charles Russel of Maynooth, one of the key figures in nineteenth century Ireland. Russel, as Newman pointed out in his Apologia, had more to do with his conversion to the Catholic Church than anyone else. The inspiration to write to Newman came suddenly on the morning of Holy Thursday after he had read Matins. The reading from Augustine on the real presence of Christ in the Eucharist moved him to think of Newman's difficulties with the doctrine of transubstantiation. Normally he was very hesitant to intrude into the affairs of others but this time he felt compelled to clear up a fellow Christian's misunderstanding of an important theological point. The formal description of the influence of the Spirit on John should not blind us to the Spirit's pervasive influence in our lives when we listen. In his fascinating book on the Holy Spirit (*The Go-Between God*, SCM, London, 1972, p 38), John V. Taylor gives a marvellous description of the enormous breadth and range of the Creator Spirit which embraces

> the plant-geneticist breeding a new strain of wheat, the World Health Organization team combating bilharzia, the reconstuction company throwing a bridge across a river barrier, the political pressure group . . . the research chemist and the worn-out school teacher in a remote village, the psychiatrist and the designer, the famine-relief worker and the computer operator, the pastor and the astronaut.

Like the Old Testament prophets, John records his call. His identification of himself resembles apocalyptic writers like Daniel (Dn 7:28). He is careful to point out that he is "their brother," with a similar threefold experience of tribulation, the kingdom, and patient endurance, because they are "in Jesus" — a phrase similar to the favourite phrase "in Christ" of Paul. It is surprising to find "the kingdom" sandwiched in between tribulation and patient endurance. Obviously, the kingdom is not just a future reality but a present experience of Jesus' loving rule in the midst of the sufferings of their lives. Endurance, says Charles in his commentary, is the spiritual alchemy which transmutes suffering into royal dignity. The phrase "in Jesus" modifies each of the three key words — to suffer tribulation is to be with Jesus who gives the strength to endure.

John's exile evidently resulted from his proclamation of "God's word and his witness to Jesus" (v 9), although he does not give any details of the charges against him. His experience "I was in the Spirit," which probably means that he was inspired or caught up in the power of the Spirit, is repeated in 4:2; 17:3; 21:10 and can be compared with the experiences recounted in Ezek 3:12 and Acts 22:17. The early Christians were firmly convinced that the Spirit of the risen Jesus was at work in their midst (2 Cor 3:12–18). To proclaim the gospel meant to speak in and under the Spirit. Here, we have the only New Testament use of the phrase "the Lord's Day," a phrase found also in Ignatius of Antioch and the Didache. It probably means Sunday the first day of the week. Quite early , the Christians celebrated the redemption of Christ with organised liturgies on Sunday (Ac 20:7; 1 Cor 16:2). One speculation is that because one day each month was set apart as "Emperor's Day," John may be making a clear contrast.

Like Isaiah's vision of old, John's fundamental vision seems to have taken place during a liturgical celebration. He hears a voice giving him a commission not to speak but to write a book. The voice may be that of Christ or rather that of the angel who frequently comes to him (4:1; 5:2). The vision extends until the end of chapter 3. As in Daniel's vision (Dn 10) two parts can be distinguished in the opening description. It begins with a hyperbolic, sevenfold description of the glorified Christ (v 12–16) and is followed by his words to John (v 17–20). This tremendous vision of the glorified Christ is intended to dominate the whole book just as the mosaics influenced by it dominated the early churches of Christianity. His concentration on the decisive role of the Messiah distinguishes John's work from contemporary Jewish apocalypses.

In these the Messiah is often not mentioned at all or at best plays a secondary role. Jewish apocalypses know nothing of the sudden coming of a messiah who has already achieved our salvation through a previous appearance.

Even a brief analysis of the description shows that one cannot imagine this vision. Rather it is a literary vision with parts drawn from texts like Zechariah 4:10 (the lampstand), Daniel 7 (like a son of man, the description of the hair), from Exodus (the robe and girdle) and Ezekiel (the feet and the voice). The Greek particle "hos" ("like," "as") found here is used altogether about 55 times in the book. It shows that the earthly terms are only approximate terms for the heavenly realities which are described. In his vision John sees seven lampstands of gold — gold was the most obvious metal to suggest splendour and glory. Perhaps his imagination recalls the "menorah" or seven branched candelabrum which stood outside the second veil of the Hebrew tabernacle (Ex 25:31–40). The seven lampstands are the seven churches (1:20) — in 2:5 we are told that failure to repent resulted in the loss of one's place as a lampstand. In Zechariah's vision the seven branched golden lampstand is explained as "the eyes of the Lord which range over the whole earth." The suggestion seems to be that the seven churches are or should be light bearers to the Son of Man, the source of their light who walks among them like God among his people in the Old Testament (Lv 26:12). The risen Jesus is magnificently symbolized as combining the image of Daniel's heavenly son of man and the Ancient of Days (hair like pure wool) who gives him his throne (Dn 7:9). We Christians have come to associate the term "son of man" with the notion of a "gentle Jesus meek and mild." But the following picture is an indication of how a Jew of the first century would have imagined the term — a heavenly judge with flaming eyes, feet like bronze and a sword in his mouth. The long robe and the golden girdle were the distinctive clothing of priests and kings (Ex 28:4).

Seven physical characteristics are described: head and hair, eyes, feet, voice, right hand, mouth, and face. The "eyes of flaming fire" probably refer to his penetrating knowledge of all mysteries. The glowing feet can overcome all opposition like hot metal burning what is in its way. The voice like "rushing waters" suggests that God's judgement drowns all in its path (Ezek 43:2). The seven stars which Jesus holds in his right hand symbolizing his powerful protection, are the heavenly counterparts of the seven churches (v 20). Stars were associated in Job 38:7 with angels. The sharp two-edged sword proceeding from his mouth, and not wielded by his hand, suggests the short Roman sword which was tongue-like in shape. The rare word for sword is found again in Lk 2:35. The image of irresistible power and judgement of Jesus is like that of Heb 4:12 where the word of God cuts more keenly than any two-edged sword (Heb 4:12; 2 Thess 2:8; Is 49:2). Like the creative Yahweh himself, his word is sufficient (Is 11:4). Finally his dazzling face is compared to "the sun at its brightest." Matthew's portrayal of the divine shining through Jesus at his transfiguration is quite similar (Mt 17:2). This tremendous picture of the divine Jesus, the eschatological judge, is not intended merely to strengthen his audience against their enemies. The following chapters show that the Christian communities themselves are also under the judging word of Jesus. The seven letters will each use one of the terms of this description of Jesus.

John's death-like collapse before the majestic vision of the Son of Man in glory can be compared to the reactions of

Ezekiel (1:28), Isaiah (6:5), Daniel (10:9), or Peter (Lk 5:8). It is the typical reaction of fear and awe in the presence of the numinous. Jesus' touch and reassuring words "stop being afraid" are familiar from the gospel. The gentle touch of Jesus contrasts sharply with the awesome figure of power which has just been sketched. Jesus describes himself with words applied to God in Isaiah 44:6 and 48:12 — "First and Last" are much the same as Alpha and Omega and mean that Jesus alone is the divine creator and the lord of all our history. Jesus who had died not only is alive forevermore but holds the keys of human destiny. He is lord of the spirit world and even of death itself (6:8). The commission to write is reaffirmed (1:19) and enlarged to include not only the present vision of Christ and its interpretation but also what he will see later. The first vision is described as a mystery. This does not mean something mysterious in the modern way of speaking. In the New Testament mystery is often used for the content of the gospel message. It is a hidden symbol which people could not fathom by themselves but which is now disclosed (Dn 2:28). In chapter 17 the mystery of the whore is that she is the great city ruling the earth. The seven stars are the presiding spirits of the seven churches and the seven lampstands are the seven churches (Dn 10:13–21). In the following seven artificial letters the wonderful figure of the vision will speak to the seven churches in a manner not unlike that of Amos' seven oracles which were also received in a vision.

C. *Seven Letters to a Very Human Church,* 2:1–3:22

In the New Testament at least three different approaches to the concrete spirituality of the different communities can be distinguished. Paul's approach is the direct method bluntly facing the issues. His letters normally begin with a positive thanksgiving or praise section and then are divided roughly into a believing and a behaving section — Paul has no problem moving from curses, threats, and sarcastic criticisms to reminders of blessings, to kindly exhortation. The approach of a Matthew is quite different, exemplifying the power of indirect storytelling at its best. Matthew has two layers to his work. The historical Jesus is speaking at one level to his contemporaries. But at a deeper, indirect level the risen Jesus is addressing the disciples, Pharisees, etc. and the problems of Matthew's own community at Antioch. The approach of the Apocalypse is somewhat in between these two. The risen Jesus is imagined as making a critique of John's contemporaries through the letters which he had dictated to John. These letters can be an excellent mirror in which we can see ourselves, our contemporary church mixture of apathy, imperfection and idealism. They provide the honest questions which any community or person should have the courage to face occasionally lest we become victims of what Dietrich Bonhoeffer (*The Cost of Discipleship*, p 45) called cheap grace:

> the grace we bestow upon ourselves ... it is the preaching of forgiveness without requiring repentance, baptism without church discipline, communion without confession. Cheap grace is grace without discipleship.

The analysis is not a scientific or sociological one giving facts and figures, but a prophetic analysis. There is no need for the author to prove, only to use his prophetic intuition and his appeal to conscience. But his message is for Christian com-

munities: his seven churches were real flesh-and-blood places.
At least five can be visited and walked through today. Of
Thyatira and Philadelphia only fourth century artifacts are
left. But the whole Apocalypse was sent to every church giving
each a wider horizon of praise and blame than is found in the
particular message it received.

Each of the letters or, rather, messages is constructed
according to the same general design in seven parts giving a
certain concentric pattern—the first and last churches are in
serious danger, the second and sixth are in very good condition
while the central three are neither very good nor very bad. The
two that received only praise are obviously quite poor and
without political and economic power. Those that receive
only censure are rich and complacent with no signs of persecution. Thus John proposes an uncompromising stand for Jesus
and his values against the dehumanising powers of the Roman
Empire and its successors in every age. The pattern of the
individual messages is as follows:

a) The church named: "To the angel of the church in
   Ephesus . . ."

b) A title of the risen Christ, a phrase drawn from the great
   vision in chapter 1.

c) A section headed "I know," giving an intimate assessment of the Church's condition — totally negative for
   Sardis and Laodicea.

d) Words of rebuke or encouragement - no criticism for
   Smyrna and Philadelphia.

e) A command of the risen Jesus to alert each to the deception involved.

f) A general exhortation "He who has an ear, let him hear ..."

g) A promise of reward for those victorious. Each is an eschatological promise and can be correlated with an aspect of the final two chapters (ch 21–22).

TO EPHESUS, 2:1–7

The first community addressed is that of Ephesus, called "The Vanity Fair of the Ancient World." Favourably located at the mouth of the Cayster River, Ephesus was the most important commercial and cultural centre in Asia Minor with about 150,000 inhabitants. The scene of a lengthy ministry of Paul (Ac 19:1–10), its Christians were the recipients of the Epistle to the Ephesians. Timothy lived there for a time (1 Tim 1:3) as also did John in his old age, according to tradition.

The greeting from the one "who holds the seven stars in his right hand" is one of reassurance, reminding the people of Jesus' controlling presence. The commendation begins with the remark that Jesus knows what is happening at Ephesus: "I know your works and labour and your patient endurance." "Works" is a general term. "Kopos" (labour) means work to the point of weariness. Paul writing to the Thessalonians mentions the same threefold activity and the threefold source of faith, love, and hope (1 Thes 1:3). In addition to dedication, their ability to discern evil in their midst and their courageous endurance of hardships are stressed. Gifted with the power to discern spirits, they had parted ways with the false apostles among them and had kept to the orthodox ways (1 Jn 4:1; 2 Cor 11:13–15). Paul in his farewell speech had warned that "grievous wolves" would disturb the church at Ephesus.

They knew that the cause of Jesus was demanding, and they were prepared to pay the price. Some fifteen years later Ignatius of Antioch wrote to the Ephesians and likewise commended them for refusing to give a home to heresy. Polycarp records an amusing story about John, who was earning his living as a bath attendant at Ephesus. One day he called to his companion to get out of the baths as quickly as possible. The heretic Cerinthus had just come in and John was afraid the building might collapse on their heads.

Given such praise to the church at Ephesus, the coming rebuke is somewhat surprising. But a comparison between the letters shows that Ephesus and Thyatira, which are rebuked, receive more praise than Smyrna and Philadelphia, which are not being rebuked. The rebuke to Ephesus is couched in a memorable phrase "you have abandoned your first love." A similar charge was brought by Jeremiah — "I remember the love of your youth, how you loved me as a bride" (Jer 2:2; Hos 2:14–16). Have we here the modern distinction among uncritical love, unloving criticism and loving criticism? Paul's reflection is also a quite apt description of a hardworking orthodox church without love:

> If I give everything I have to feed the poor and hand over my body to be burned, but have not love, I gain nothing. (1 Cor 13:3).

They had lost that "first fine careless rapture." To try to distinguish whether love of God or love of people or love of the community is at stake is beside the point. In Ephesus there was a history of hostility between Jew and Gentile. It was famous for its magical charms or "Ephesian letters," its emperor-worship, and its great temple of Artemis, one of the seven wonders of the world. In their zeal to combat all these temptations the Ephesians needed to ask themselves questions like those expressed by the poet William Cowper:

> Where is the blessedness I knew
> When first I met the Lord?
> Where is that soul-refreshing view
> of Jesus and His Word?

The exhortation consists of three brief commands: "keep remembering, repent, and do the first works," which provide a good summary of a true conversion experience. The idea of a "command" morality causes many difficulties today when the emphasis is on the role of freedom of conscience in religion and on the dignity of the human person. However, the Bible does not see Christian morality as merely flowing from our enlightened understanding. It is a faith morality whose main source is the Word of God, which is as revealing as it is imperative. The temptation of Adam, as of every person, is not to trust that the guidance of the commandments comes from a good God concerned with our best interests. According to John's Gospel only the person who obeys God's word is truly free (Jn 8:31f).

The story of the Old Testament is the story of forgetfulness. Despite the continual advice of such books as Deuteronomy (Dt 4:9) the people forgot their Yahweh and were led into sin (Jer 2:13; Hos 2:15; Jgs 8:34). The Old Testament stress on remembering is continued into the New Testament.

Luke in particular puts great stress on this in his parables, his hymns in the central act of Christian worship (22:19), and in such texts as 23:42; 24:6–9. Memory, in the biblical sense, is to cross the barriers of space and time, to make present, alive, and active a past event or person. John likewise asks the community at Sardis, "Do you remember how eager you were when you first heard the message?" (3:3). The Ephesians are bluntly told that they have fallen! They have forgotten the love of Jesus.

True remembrance leads to repentance — the tense suggests a sharp, immediate action. Repentance is a key aim of our writer. The Greek word suggests a change of thinking, of values, of emphasis. The Hebrew background is that of turning back to God — God is love and to turn from him is to lose love. True repentance issues in deeds of love.

The alternative is the coming of Jesus in judgement and the removal of their lampstand. Examples of once bright churches no longer a light to the world are easy to find. Ephesus, like Capernaum, is just a ruin today.

But all is not negative at Ephesus. Their hatred of the practices of the Nicolaitans (not of the people themselves) is like that of Jesus himself. Our information about the Nicolaitans is quite vague. Irenaeus linked them with the proselyte Nicolaus, one of the Seven (Ac 6:5). He further claimed that John's gospel was written to combat similar teaching from the Gnostic Cerinthus who claimed special knowledge of the divine. An examination of the text suggest a relationship to the Balaamites (2:14–16) and Jezebel (2:20): the practice of eating food sacrificed to idols, and immoral habits. The first commentator on the Apocalypse, Victorinus of Pettau, describes the Nicolaitans as

false and troublesome men who as ministers under the name of
Nicolaus, had made for themselves a heresy, to the effect that
what had been offered to idols might be exorcised and eaten
and that whoever had committed fornication might receive
peace on the eighth day.

An interesting suggestion is that John's aim is to encourage
Christian exclusiveness against "the enemy within," the
inroads of the pagan culture with which they were being
swamped because of their political, economic, and social
activities.

Each letter concludes with an exhortation to listen to the
Spirit. In recent years the problem of hearing without listening
has come very much to the fore, as is evident from the popular
poster:

I know you believe you understand what you think I said. But I
am not sure you realise that what you heard is not what I
meant.

This exhortation clearly recalls similar statements attributed
to Jesus in the gospels (Mk 4:9; Mt 11:15; 13:9). It puts the
emphasis and responsibility clearly on the shoulders of the
individual, although the letter is sent to the churches and not
even to Ephesus alone. Hitherto Christ was the speaker; now
it is the Spirit who is speaking. A similar relationship is found
in Rom 8:9.

The concluding promise for Ephesus is that the conqueror
will eat of the tree of life in the paradise of God. All these
promises are fulfilled in the final chapters (22:2). In Jewish
apocalyptic writings the age of the Messiah is described as a

return to the conditions of the garden of Eden. For example, the Testament of Levi (18:10–11) promises that the gates of paradise will be opened, the sword threatening Adam will be removed, God will give the saints to eat from the tree of life and the spirit of holiness will be upon them.

The promise is to the one who conquers not others but evil so as to find an enduring life of love. As the commentator, Swete, points out,

> The note of victory is dominant in St. John, as that of faith in St. Paul; or rather, faith presents itself to St. John in the light of a victory.

The imagery is similar to that of the beatitudes in the Sermon on the Mount with its emphasis on the importance of love.

TO SMYRNA, 2:8–11

Smyrna (modern Izmir) with its excellent harbour lay some 40 miles due north of Ephesus and competed with it for the title of premier city in the province of Asia in commerce, culture, and Roman influence. Of the seven messages this one is the most complimentary. It is full of contrasting extremes: first/last, became dead/came to life, poverty/abundance, say they are Jews/but are not, death/crown of life. Local allusion can be detected as well. The title of Jesus, "first and last, who died and came to life," suggests Smyrna's claim to be "first of Asia in beauty and emperor loyalty." It also suggests the fact that Smyrna lay destroyed for three to four hundred years. In competition with eleven other cities, Smyrna in A.D. 23 won from the Roman Senate the privilege of building the first temple in honour of the Emperor Tiberius. Worship, the equivalent of political loyalty, involved the burning of incense and the statement, "Caesar is Lord." But in a city zealous for emperor worship, it is not surprising to find a record of Christian martyrs who refused to conform. The historian Eusebius records the burning alive of the twelfth martyr in Smyrna, the eighty-six year old Polycarp, about the year A.D. 156. His famous words have resounded ever since:

> Eighty-six years I have served Christ, and he has never done me wrong. How can I blaspheme my King who saved me?

Conflict with the large local Jewish community was blamed for this martyrdom.

In the rather vague commendation to the church at Smyrna, victorious tribulation, poverty, and slander are singled out. The word for tribulation, "thlipsis," literally means pressure and can mean anything which presses upon the Christian ranging from want and difficult circumstances to sorrow and loneliness, persecution and unpopularity. In the Greek Old Testament it was used of the oppression in Egypt (Ex 4:31) and in the Exile (Dt 4:29). The prophets used it for the divine visitation of God's people (Is 37:3–4; Nahum 1:7). In Daniel 12:1, a remarkable passage showing the growing belief in the afterlife, the present tribulation was only a preparation for the final day of tribulation. But then Michael, the patron angel of Israel, would come and deliver everyone who had remained faithful and whose name was written in the book of life (12:7).

The strong word "Ptōcheia" (poverty) can be applied to material as well as spiritual poverty or a spirit of piety as opposed to pride. The community at Qumran identified itself as the poor of Yahweh who would be preserved through tribulation. The question is, why they were poor in a city renowned for its prosperity. Probably their attitude towards emperor worship led to their being excluded from the corridors of economic power. In reality they are rich, possessing what Matthew described as treasure in heaven (Mt 6:19–21; 2 Cor 8:9).

The blasphemy or slander of those who call themselves Jews but are not probably refers to the early Christian view that Christians were the true spiritual Israelites and the real children of Abraham (Rom 2:25ff; Gal 6:15f). The word "synagogue" stands in sharp contrast to the word "church" used of the Christian community. The actual phrase "synagogue of Satan" is found only once more in ancient literature (3:9). This is the first mention of the devil in the book. He is one of the main actors in the whole drama, the ultimate source of their persecution. One suggestion is that these false Jews were a particular group who had developed a syncretistic religion by combining pagan practices with their own. At any rate, only some Jews were involved and there is no suggestion that all Jewish synagogues were synagogues of Satan.

Like Matthew in his missionary sermon (Mt 10:28) John advises his readers that they should not be afraid of suffering. He then stresses the final death, judgement, and banishment from God's presence, things about which they should really be concerned. The "second death" is a phrase found in the Targumic commentaries such as Moses' prayer, which is an expansion of Dt 33:6:

> Let Reuben live in this world, and not die in the second death,
> in which death the wicked die in the world to come.

The imprisonment will only last ten days, a semitism for a
brief period (Neh 4:12; Dn 1:2). Ancient prisons were not
punitive like ours but rather a holding place until the trial took
place. Therefore he invites them to be faithful even to the
point of death. Perhaps there is an allusion to the history of
Smyrna here, an invitation to be as faithful to Christ as they
were to the Romans. Cicero described Smyrna as the most
faithful of the Roman allies, faithful even in the days before
Rome's power was widely acknowledged in the region. Victory would naturally lead to a garland or wreath, not just the
crown of the victorious athletes but the crown of life, the gift
of Christ (20:6; 22:5; Ps 21:4; Is 28:5). Ancient writers
celebrated the "crown of Smyrna" because its hill, Pagos, had a
rounded top crowned with beautiful buildings. A Qumran
text describes this glorious crown to be worn by the faithful
(1QS 4:6–8):

> And as for the Visitation of all who walk in this (Spirit), it
> consists of healing and abundance of bliss, with length of days
> and fruitfulness and all blessings without end, and eternal joy
> in perpetual life, and the glorious crown and the garment of
> honor in everlasting life.

TO PERGAMUM, 2:12–17

Pergamum, whence our word "parchment" is derived, was
about 65 miles to the north of Smyrna. The nominal capital of
the Roman province of Asia (Ephesus was in fact the most
important city), it was the most important centre of emperor-
worship in the eastern part of the empire. A temple was
erected to Roma and Augustus in 27 B.C. on a sharply

protruding hill which dominates the surrounding countryside and gives a view as far as the Isle of Lesbos. Thus one can understand the reference to the Roman proconsul's head-quarters as "Satan's throne," though some would explain the reference in terms of the great altars of Zeus. The power of the Roman sword is subtly contrasted with the sword of the divine word of the risen Christ. Balaam who is mentioned in v 14 was actually slain by a sword (Num 31:8). Pergamum was one of the rare cities to which Rome had given "the right of the sword," the power to exercise capital punishment. The two main religions seem to have been the worship of Dionysus, symbolized by the bull, and Asclepius, the god of healing symbolized by the snake. R.H. Charles calls Pergamum the Lourdes of the ancient world, because it was a famous place of pilgrimage for the sick.

The Christians of Pergamum are praised for holding fast to Christ's name (not to Caesar's). In the Hebrew and ancient world a name was no superficial label but an indication of the personality, characteristics, and essential function of a person. Despite their enduring faith in a hostile world, even in the face of the martyrdom of the faithful witness Antipas, they are criticised for giving in to heterodoxy. Nothing further is known about Antipas (2:13) who receives the same title of "faithful witness" as Christ himself (1:5). Legend says that he was roasted in a brazen bull. Perhaps his name, which means "against all," is symbolic. The community was divided because some were following the hated teaching of the Balaam-ites and Nicolaitans (2:6). Curiously the name Balaam in Hebrew can be interpreted as to "conquer the people," a meaning which the word Nicolaitans can also have. If this is so, both groups may be closely related. The Old Testament story of Balaam and the memorable incident at Baal-peor is a story of deception, perhaps the activity most associated with Satan. Balak the Moabite king had failed to get the venal prophet Balaam to curse the Hebrews directly. But Balaam instead advised Balak on the way to put a "skandalon" or stumbling block to trap the Israelites. Balaam knew that the Israelites would forfeit Yahweh's protection if they could be induced to worship idols (Num 25:1; 31:16). Thus he got the Moabite women to seduce the Israelites and induce them to sacrifice to their god, Baal-peor. Israel was punished for its fornication and idolatry.

The sins mentioned at Pergamum are "eating meats sacrificed to idols and fornication," two of the four practices forbidden to Gentile converts by the quite broadminded Council of Jerusalem (Ac 15:20). This phrase may refer to the ancient custom of sharing in the temple sacrifice and of having sexual intercourse with the cult priestess-prostitutes (1 Cor 10:19–22; 1 Jn 5:21). Throughout the Bible immorality and idolatry are frequently synonymous. The question was not one of merely eating meat at a friend's house that was once sacrificed in a pagan temple. The act of eating meat was often seen as an act of worship of another god. The symbolism was important.

The blunt advice to Pergamum is to repent. The alternative is that Jesus will fight against them — a verb found outside the Apocalypse only in James 4:2 — with the sword of his mouth, his all powerful word of judgement. The choice is theirs and the punishment self-inflicted. A similar threat is found in a Qumran allusion to Is 11:4 where the Prince of the Congregation is admonished to strike the people with the might of his mouth:

You will devastate the earth with the sceptre and by the breath of your mouth the ungodly.

This is the warrior-Messiah whose approach can be traced as far back as Miriam's victory song (Ex 15:21).

The challenge to listen and conquer is enhanced by the promise of a threefold reward of the hidden manna, a white stone and a new name. The gift of manna contrasts with the food of the idols. In Jewish tradition some of the manna had been stored in the ark (Ex 16:32–34). But when the temple was destroyed in 587 B.C. an angel of Jeremiah had hidden the ark with its manna until the time when the Messianic kingdom would arrive (2 Mc 2:5; 2 Bar 29:8). The message is that the risen Lord will give heavenly food to the believer (Jn 4:31–33; Heb 9:4). The meaning of the white stone and the new name has been a source of much discussion among commentators. Perhaps the solidity of a stone is contrasted with the perishable nature of parchment — a play on the word Pergamum. In the ancient world a stone was used as a voting ballot or a ticket to public functions and free meals. Also when drawing lots in a criminal case a white stone was the sign of a favourable judgement, a sign of life. Many other interpretations are suggested: a symbol of a happy day, a good luck amulet, the precious stones expected to fall from heaven with the manna, a stone in the high priest's breastplate with the name of one of the chosen tribes written upon it. The best interpretation suggests an entrance ticket to paradise, to the heavenly banquet.

Romano Guardini once interpreted the promise of a new name as the fulfillment of our personal existence when everyone is completely him or herself, irrevocably unique and free. The particular word "new" is applied to a song, to Jerusalem, heaven and earth and all things in the Apocalypse. The word suggests quality and freshness rather than recency. A name in the ancient world reflected the personality or function or essence. Another interpretation is that the new name is Christ's own name which is offered as a protective shield to all who trust in him (Is 62:2). The giving of a new name symbolized that the person was in the power of the one naming. Perhaps there is a reference to the title "Augustus," the new name deliberately devised by the Roman senate for Octavian.

TO THYATIRA, 2:18-29

Thyatira, a garrison city on the eastern frontier of the Roman province of Asia, some 45 miles southeast of Pergamum, was the least important of the seven cities. Yet it receives the longest letter. Not much is known about Thyatira, although the archaeologist Sir William Ramsay says that more trade guilds are known from inscriptions in Thyatira than in any other Asian city. Each guild had its own patron gods, feasts, and revelries. According to Acts 16:14, a woman name Lydia, a dealer in purple goods from Thyatira, opened her house to Paul at Philippi.

Two of the details in the description of Christ's eyes and feet come from the inaugural vision (1:14-15). However, the term "the son of God" is found only here in the Apocalypse, although it is implicit in such texts as 1:6; 2:27; 3:5,21; 14:1. Probably the author uses it here because the messianic Psalm 2 is being quoted in v 27. Perhaps, too, he is reacting against the custom of calling the emperor the son of God. There is some evidence from Qumran that the title Son of God was used in pre-Christian times by Aramaic speakers in Palestine and that it was not the creation of the missionary propaganda. However, this is not to say that there was an expectation of a divine Messiah, but of an adopted son of Yahweh as is found in Psalm 2. The use in Qumran refers either to a priestly or political Messiah or perhaps to some supernatural figure like Michael or Melchizedek.

The emphasis on the blazing fire of Christ' eyes may be a contrast to the worship of the sun god, Apollo.

Christ's knowledge and commendation of the church in Thyatira focuses on "their works" which are fivefold: love, faith, service, patient endurance, and a progress that contrasts with the regression at Ephesus. Curiously Thyatira receives much greater praise than Smyrna and Philadelphia which receive no negative criticism at all.

The problem is overtolerance of a self-appointed prophetess named Jezebel. The name is evidently symbolic because, given Jezebel's proverbial association with wickedness, no self-respecting Jewess would have borne such a name. The historic Jezebel was the daughter of the king of Sidon who married Ahab, king of Israel. She aggressively introduced foreign ways into Israel. She even attempted violently to wipe out Yahwism, causing her husband to worship Baal to the horror of the prophet Elijah (1 Kgs 16–18). The practices are probably the same as those of the Nicolaitans and those seduced by Balaam. Many agree with R.H. Charles' suggestion that the tolerance was due to the acceptance of membership in the city guilds and the common meals. The aim of the Apocalypse is towards a much greater exclusiveness than that which Paul tolerated at Corinth (1 Cor 5:1–9). The question is basically one which concerns every generation. It has been well described, from Paul's letter to the man with this name, as Philemon's problem. Since the cultural situation, the social, political, and economic orders, never conform adequately to the ideals of the gospel, how far can Christians go in conforming to the world around them without falling into apathy and complacency?

Thyatira's sin is even worse because Jezebel had received a previous warning but had refused to repent (Mt 18:17), even though she had been given time to do so. The punishment which fits the crime is described in the vivid present tense —

> Behold I am hurling her on her couch (not of love but) of sickness.

Sin often was believed to result in sickness and with good reason. Her lovers and her children or her followers "I will strike dead," a strong phrase meaning, perhaps, a pestilence. But the prospect of forgiveness is held out "if they do repent." While the whole book is full of seemingly harsh judgements, the prospect of salvation is continually emphasised. The purpose of the punishment is deterrence:

> All the churches will know that I am he who searches the kidneys and the heart.

The kidneys in Hebrew thinking represent the seat of the emotions, and the heart the inner life of the intelligence and will. Nothing is hidden from Christ's all seeing gaze (Heb 4:12–13). He will judge all impartially according to their deeds (Rom 2:6,16).

The community is clearly divided. There is special advice for those who do not follow Jezebel's teaching and who do not know "the deep things of Satan as they call them," to cling to what they have "until I come." The emphasis on putting no further burden on them reminds us of the apostolic decree in Acts 15:28f.

The remark about "the deep things of Satan as they say" is somewhat vague but it probably is a sarcastic reference to the practices of Jezebel. In 1 Cor 2:10 (Rom 11:33), Paul refers to the deep things of God revealed by the Spirit. Some second century libertine Gnostic groups claimed to know the deep things of Satan and to be able to conquer him by taking part in the pagan rites. The approach of Jezebel and her followers may have been to claim freedom or even advantages in their experiences (1 Cor 8:9–11). The first promise to this small community, of authority over the nations which Jesus received from the Father, must have seemed somewhat fantastic. The reference is to the messianic Psalm 2 which was used in the pre-Christian *Psalms of Solomon* to describe the coming reign of the Messiah and the faithful Jews. In Psalm 2 the idea of shepherding those who follow with the iron-tipped rod of the shepherd may be intended to contrast with the breaking in pieces of those who resist. A custom in Egyptian and Mesopotamian coronation rituals was publicly and ritually to smash pots with the names of their enemies written on them. The breaking of a pot symbolized a destruction that was total, effortless, and irreparable.

The promise of the morning star, which is the same as the evening star and the planet Venus, is the gift of Christ himself (22:16; 2 Pt 1:19). The morning star is the herald of the dawn after darkness, a symbol of hope. Jesus is the rising of the new day of eternity. The churches are only reflecting lamps and angels are only ordinary stars, but Jesus is the bright morning star in the freshness of the new life. A military saviour in Israel was described in Num 24:27 as a rising star. The influence of rising stars may be behind the imagery here.

TO SARDIS, 3:1–6

Sardis, a busy commercial and industrial town at the junction of five roads some thirty miles south of Thyatira, had been the capital of ancient Lydia with its ill-fated king Croesus. Levelled by an earthquake in 17 B.C., it had been rebuilt and, under the Romans, had recovered somewhat from its decline. But as the archaeologist Ramsay pointed out,

> No city of Asia at that time showed such a melancholy contrast between past splendour and present decay.

Although no specific sins are singled out, Sardis receives no commendation but almost as severe a rebuke as does Laodicea: "in fact you are dead despite your reputation of being alive." It seems reasonable to conclude that this prophetic critique penetrated the people's apathy and luxury in a way that is not evident to the superficial view. As long ago as the fifth century the Greek historian Herodotus criticised the people of Sardis as

> tender-footed Lydians, who can only play on the cithera, strike the guitar, and sell by retail.

The modern commentator G.B. Caird speculates thus about the city:

> Content with mediocrity, lacking both the enthusiasm to entertain a heresy and the depth of conviction which provokes intolerance, it was too innocuous to be worth persecuting.

A key question which continually demands reflection in the history of Christianity is: how does a Church die? In Hebrew the word death means the loss of one's spiritual vitality. The contrast between dead and alive recalls Luke's statement that the Prodigal Son was dead and has come to life or James' remark that faith without good works is dead (Jam 2:17,26). Paul, curiously, does not mention death in Galatians but, particularly in Romans, he connects the flesh, sin, and death: "If you live according to the flesh you will die " (Rom 8:1). Death, the wages of sin, is already a reality (Rom 3:23). The reference to death may be a play on the fact that some seven miles from Sardis there was quite an impressive necropolis. Evidently death was of special interest to the Sardians.

Four admonitions are given: wake up, strengthen what remains before it dies, keep remembering what you received, and repent. The warning to wake up, to be constantly alert, has particular relevance in the light of the history of Sardis (Rom 13:11; 1 Cor 16: 13). The citadel of Sardis was located on an almost impregnable hill with almost vertical walls on three sides. Yet the city was taken by suprise on two occasions by Croesus in 549 B.C. and by Antiochus the Great in 195 B.C. in a night attack. Their deeds are criticised for being "incomplete in the sight of my God," a reference more to the quality than the quantity of their lives. There is an urgency about the advice. Unlike the Philadelphians (3:8), the Sardians are not holding onto the word which they received, the apostolic tradition. Unless they change, Jesus will come like a thief at an unexpected hour, a reference not to the parousia (Mt 24:43; 1 Thes 5:2; 2 P 3:10), which will take place whether we are awake or not, but to a preliminary punishment.

But there are few "names" who are faithful, who have not defiled their garments. Neither, it should be observed, are they called martyrs. There were other problems in the communities besides emperor worship. Some votive inscriptions from Asia Minor show that those who wore dirty garments were excluded from worship because they were an insult to the gods. But the meaning here is probably symbolic, with clothes symbolising personality or reputation. In Zech 3:3–5 Joshua's clean and dirty garments symbolise his innocence or his guilt. Although their outward reputation was good, their inner hearts were not what they should have been. Soiled or dirty symbolises mixing with a pagan way of life and failing to keep the Christian exclusivism which the author required (1 Cor 8:7; Jude v 23). The promise to the few is that they will "walk with Christ in white because they are worthy." The reference to clothes possibly derives from the famous wool-dying industry in Sardis. Members of such sects as Qumran wore white garments as a symbol of their interior purity. White was the colour used by the Roman Emperor in a triumphal procession. In the Old Testament white garments signify heaven (Dn 7:9), victory (2 Mac 11:8), festivity (Qoh 9:8). All these symbols are included here with the emphasis on victory.

A white garment was frequently used in baptismal texts as an image of the salvation already achieved by Christ and begun in the newly baptised. This reference to white clothing is developed into the threefold promise of white garments, their names not erased from the book of life, but acknowledged "before my Father and his angels." Each promise involves a corresponding warning. In ancient cities the names of citizens were kept in registers and were erased upon death. The idea of writing in the book of life had a long history in Judaism. Moses asked to be blotted out of the book of life, if the Israelites, after the golden calf episode, were not forgiven. By the time of Daniel 12:1 (Lk 10:20; Phil 4:3; Heb 12:23) the theme had developed to include the idea of life after death, of belonging to Christ's kingdom even after death (Rom 8:38–39). Later in 17:8 John speaks of predestination but a predestination conditional on faith and faithfulness.

The final promise is a paraphrase of Jesus' pronouncement that he would acknowledge those who confess him (Mt 10:32; Lk 12:8). It is a challenge to the readers to confess Jesus' name on earth.

TO PHILADELPHIA, 3:7–13

Philadelphia (modern Alasehir) was about twenty five miles south-east of Sardis. Described as the last bastion of Asian Christianity, it survived as a free city until 1392, to the admiration of historians like Gibbon. Today there is a resident bishop there and five churches. The name, which means brotherly love, was derived from its founder Attalus II who was called Philadelphus because of his love for his brother. He founded this strong fortress city to be a "little Athens," a centre of Greek culture and a "gateway to the East," a mission city spreading the Greek language and culture among the barbarian Phrygians. Because of its rich volcanic soil suitable for grape growing, the local wine industry flourished. The Christian community was small (v 8) and, as there is no mention of heresy or factions, its enemies were from the outside. No blame is given and, as at Smyrna, only praise is mentioned.

The encouraging greeting to a small community is from the holy and true one who has the keys of David. Holiness and Truthfulness are attributes of Yahweh, who is called the Holy One and the God of Truth in the Old Testament (Hos 11:9; Ex 34:6). God's powerful presence is that of the "wholly other" (Mk 1:24; 1 Jn 2:20). God is the one who is completely trustworthy in word and in action. The possession of the keys (1:8) indicates the messianic authority to admit or exclude from the kingdom. The background text is given to the faithful Eliakim instead of to the unfaithful Shebna. The handing over of the keys signifies not the appointment of a mere porter but of one authorised to exercise complete power in the house. In 9:1; 20:1 the key to the abyss gives the power to harass its impious inhabitants and to bind the dragon.

The praise of the works of the Philadelphians is threefold. Despite their little power they have been given an open door which no one is able to close, they are faithful, and they have not denied Christ's name. Between the statements "I know your deeds" and "you have little power" the statement "Behold I have put before you an open door . . ." is somewhat awkwardly placed. The literal meaning of the words by themselves suggests that Christ, the all-powerful holder of the keys from the Father, has opened a door for them which no hostile power can close. It seems natural to go further and say that because of their little power Christ himself will open problematic doors. But an open door to what? Considering Philadelphia's advantageous position as the cultural gateway to Phrygia, a suggestion has been made that missionary activity is involved (Ac 14:26). But there is little emphasis on missionary activity in the Apocalypse and the context seems to suggest some kind of reward. Another rather forced suggestion is that the door is Christ himself as in Jn 10:7ff. In 4:1 the door is into the heavenly court. This seems the best approach. Jesus will save them in spite of their little power and their difficulties with Satan's synagogue.

Further, Jesus will make these Satanic opponents fall at their feet and learn of Jesus' love for his community. John is not the last to call his opponents sons of Satan. This is a traditional approach to enemies of God in Jewish apocalypses. The criticism of the pseudo-Jews is similar to that made at Smyrna (3:10). But is John suggesting that those pseudo-Jews will be converted? In the Old Testament the hope was that the Gentiles would learn to respect Israel, come to Jerusalem and worship their God (Is 43:4). Here the (mixed) Christian community takes the place of the Jewish people. The thought seems to be similar to Paul's hope that eventually every knee will bow to Jesus the Lord, some more easily and more quickly than others (Phil 2:10). Because they have stood fast Jesus promises them protection through the hour of trial which is coming on the whole world to test the dwellers on the earth — the latter phrase is used some five more times by the writer and generally refers to non-Christians. The phrase "the hour of trial" and the kind of salvation that Jesus promises, are much disputed. There is a play on words, i.e. "keep those who have 'kept' his word." The allusion to the Our Father seems obvious. The best meaning seems to be not that they will escape suffering, but that Christ will keep them free from failing in temptation. The period involved coincides with the three and one half years of the rule of the Antichrist (13:5–10; Mk 13:19–20; Dn 12:1).

"I am coming quickly" is a typical apocalyptic message of assurance and comfort (2:25). The basic message is not only that everything is under God's guidance but that he will intervene in times of distress to turn all unto victory. The reference is probably to the final coming of Jesus as the final verses naturally move on to consider the new Jerusalem. They should, therefore, hold fast to what they have so that no one will take away their crown (2:10). Yahweh himself was described as the crown of his people (Is 28:5; Prov 12:4). The high priest had a crown with the inscription "holy to Yahweh" (Ex 29:6). According to the rabbinic tradition, the Israelites were each crowned with two crowns when they accepted the covenant and said "We will do" and "We will be obedient." But these crowns were snatched away by a horde of devils to be restored in the messianic age.

The conclusion is the same basic promise to the victors of eternal life as that found in the other letters. In these last verses there is a sevenfold emphatic use of the personal pronoun I/my. Salvation is Jesus' achievement and gift. There is also a threefold combination of names inscribed on the pillar: the name of my God, the name of the city of Jerusalem, my own new name. These will be important in the later chapters of the book (7:3; 14:1,11; 19:12; 22:4). Four times in these verses the phrase "my God" is repeated for emphasis, a phrase which shows that they are God's own special possession and under his protection (Num 6:27). The idea of making the victor a pillar in the temple is clearly symbolic because later John will insist that there is no need for a temple in God's city (21:22). Philadelphia was a city constantly in danger of earthquakes. The allusion may be to the fact that very often only some of the large temple columns were left standing in a devastated city. The idea is one of permanence and solidity, of feeling at home in the presence of the great God and never being ushered out.

There was also at Philadelphia the custom of inscribing the names of important citizens and their fathers on statues and pillars in the temples (Gal 2:9). The triple name is not that of the Trinity but of God, the new Jerusalem, and Jesus. The reference to the new Jerusalem coming down out of heaven was a text beloved of the Montanists who literally expected a new Jerusalem from heaven (Gal 4:26; Heb 12:22). It is a symbol of the new community of Jesus (21:2f). To have the name of a city is a sign of citizenship in the city. The idea of a new name perhaps refers to the fact that Philadelphia twice received new names, Neocaesarea in gratitude to Tiberius' help in rebuilding after an earthquake, and Flavia, the family name of the Emperor Vespasian. The "new name" of Christ may be the name known only to Christ himself (19:12). Perhaps it is the name "Lord," the name of the risen Christ in whose power the faithful already share.

TO LAODICEA, 3:14–22

Affluent Laodicea, known for its commercial centre, its banking, its clothing made of local black wool, and its famous medical school, was situated at the junction of three important roads, some forty-five miles southeast of Philadelphia and a hundred miles east of Ephesus. This church is mentioned four times in the Epistle to the Colossians, a letter concerned with the mixture of Jewish and mystery religion elements in the church.

As in the other letters the speaker is introduced by a brief description which accents his mysterious divine-human personality (1:5; 19:11). Here we are given the surprising title "the Amen" and the further clarification for those who did not understand Hebrew, "the faithful and true witness, the 'arche' of God's creation." The root meaning of Amen is "trustworthy." The implication of this opening text is the question: how trustworthy are the Laodiceans, how faithful is their witness? The background text alluded to may be Isaiah 65:16: "He who blesses himself in the land will bless himself by the God of Amen, and he who takes an oath in the land will bless himself by the God of Amen, and he who takes an oath in the land will swear by the God who is trustworthy." Jesus is the perfect Amen of God, the perfect witness to his plan of creation and redemption. Another text which may have influenced the writer is Proverbs 14:5,25, leading to the possible translation: "Thus says the master worker, the faithful and true witness, the foremost of his creation." But the idea is not that Christ was created. Rather, he has authority and influence over all creation.

Spiritual writers and advisers of every age have waxed eloquent on the famous statements "neither hot nor cold ..." with its disdain of lukewarmness and its ideal of total commitment in Christian witness. To be superficially a Christian but untouched by its fire is more disastrous than to be openly antagonistic. However a more precise interpretation of the text shows that the actual comparison is between the unacceptable conditions of lukewarmness and the acceptable condition that is like a hot or cold spring or drink. The word "lukewarm" found only here in biblical Greek, is found in other writers such as Arethus to describe a person who after baptism has quenched the Holy Spirit. It is used in Gregory for one who has lost the fervour of his conversion, in Origen not for a lapsed Christian but for an unregenerate person. Laodicea, despite its wealth, had a very inadequate water supply, so insipid that it often provoked vomiting. While no detailed faults of the Laodicean community are mentioned, its condition appears to be the worst of the whole seven. The charges are general: lukewarmness, arrogance, and blindness. They are all the more serious because of their insidiousness.

The deeper problem, as Christ ironically portrays, is their lack of self-criticism, their proud blindness to the real state of their affairs. Their lukewarmness does not apply so much to their complacent laxity as to their lack of realization that it is the presence of the Risen Saviour which is the source of real salvation and wealth. Their "I" approach ("You keep saying: I am rich, I have acquired wealth and need nothing") shows proud, smug self-complacency. Is their boast of material or spiritual riches? "Material" seems to be the most natural way to take the text. This fits in well with the condemnation of wealth in chapter 18 and the theory that the writer was a wandering prophet who idealized poverty. Their reality he bluntly and severely describes as wretchedness par excellence (Charles) and the need for mercy because they are "poor, blind and naked." This description seems clearly to be ridiculing the achievements at Laodicea in banking, medicine, and clothing manufacture. Their spiritual poverty contrasts with the spiritual richness at Smyrna (2:9). Luke's blessings on the poor and woes to the rich are an interesting parallel (Lk 6:20–26). They are likewise addressed to a Christian community and criticise the community's worldly wisdom and popular respect for financial achievement and security.

But the condition is not necessarily terminal. In keeping with the hopeful tone of the whole book, the author offers the commands of Christ which correspond precisely to their threefold self-deceptions. Paul Minear in *I Saw a New Earth* (p 57) comments as follows:

> The only cure for poverty-stricken disciples was to purchase from Christ gold which is refined in the agonies of the shared passion. For their nakedness (did Hans Christian Andersen find here the theme of *The Emperor's New Clothes*?) the only recourse was to buy such clothes as the naked Christ had worn on the cross. The blindness of self-deception could be cured only by understanding the correlation between Christ's love and his discipline. These three purchases constitute a substantial definition of the kind of zeal and repentance which was the burden of all John's prophecies. The thrust of these commands moves in the direction of rigorous warning. They are tantamount to saying "Open your eyes" and "Carry your cross." This letter argues against the assertion of many interpreters to the effect that John's chief concern was to provide consolation to a persecuted church. Nearer the mark would be the opposite assertion that John like Jesus was concerned to bring not peace but a sword.

The riches of Laodicea, in contrast to Sardis, are seen in the fact that after the destructive earthquake which they suffered

in A.D. 61 they spurned the offer of Roman aid. Only from
Jesus can they purchase genuine gold which will pass the test
of the divine refining fire (Zech 13:9). The white garments
contrast with the black wools for which the city was famous.
Nakedness was the ultimate humiliation and sign of poverty
in the ancient world and an abomination before God (Ex
20:26; Is 47:1–3; 2 Cor 5:2–3). Clothes in Genesis are a
symbol of God's caring solicitude for failing and rebellious
people (Gen 3:21; Ezek 16:8–14). The reference to eye-
ointment alludes to the world-renowned ointment called
"Phrygian powder" which was produced at Laodicea. That
Jesus alone gives true vision is the message (Jn 9:39).

Somewhat abruptly, the author changes from his rather
harsh denunciation to an approach of affection and tender
concern for the community which deserves it least. Alluding
to Proverbs 3:12 he insists that his chastisement comes from
his love (Heb 11:7–8). Correction if properly accepted should
lead to enthusiasm or zeal and repentance.

In the famous picture of Jesus knocking at the door we find
a very simple but profound picture of grace and free will in
action. This scene has been unforgettably captured by
Holman Hunt in his famous paintings in Kolbe College,
Oxford and in St. Paul's Cathedral, London. Christ is knocking but there is no handle on the outside of the door. The
image also reminds one of the East African custom where
visitors do not knock but instead call out "hodi" — only a
thief knocks, and runs away if he hears a response.

Some commentators, starting from Matthew 24:33 and
James 5:9, interpret the door as the coming of Christ to the
individual at the parousia. But a careful reading shows that the
author's concern is rather with the whole community in their

here-and-now response. Others see the door as opening into the hearts of the community or rather half-committed Christians. This is probably correct. However, the context shows that the community is likely a fairly self-righteous Christian community which lacks true depth in their conversion and acceptance of Christ. The author would surely approve of the famous ironical scene in C.S. Lewis' *The World's Last Night* (p 69f). The chief demon Screwtape is proposing a toast to the graduating class from the Tempter's Training College. He begins by praising the carefully chosen wine blended from different strains of hypocrisy and reaches a climax with the words "It will be an ill day for us if what most humans mean by religion ever vanishes from the earth. Nowhere do we tempt so successfully as on the very steps of the altar."

One can find a parallel to the scene in the invitation to dine in the Song of Songs 5:2 —

> I was sleeping, but my heart kept vigil,
> I heard my lover knocking:
> Open to me, my sister, my beloved,
> my dove, my perfect one.

A Christian audience would not fail to see Eucharistic overtones in the statement "I will enter his house and have supper with him and he with me" (Lk 12:36; 22:29f). The meal referred to was the main meal of the day which was a rather unhurried affair. According to R.H. Charles, "Participation" in the common meal was for the Oriental a proof of confidence and affection. The intimate fellowship of the faithful with God and the Messiah in the coming age was frequently symbolized by such a metaphor." The victor is promised a seat with Christ who had set the pattern in his own life and, after his victory, taken his seat in joint reign with his Father (Sir 47:11; Mk 16:19; Jn 16:33). The theme of joint reign with Jesus was already referred to in 1:6ff and will be continued in 5:10 and 20:4–6. The reference to the sharing of the heavenly throne leads naturally into the next chapter which imagines the heavenly throne scene. The word throne is used in every chapter except 9,10,15,17, and 18. In 2:13 and 16:10 it refers to the throne of Satan and the beast. J. Massyngbaerde Ford concludes that the main theme of the book is the dominion of God versus the dominion of Satan.

D. The "in-between" Time of the Church, 4:1–16:21

1) AN INTRODUCTORY VISION OF THE COURT OF HEAVEN, 4:1–5:15

The Apocalypse is a book describing the tension between what is and what must soon take place (1:1). The vision of the glorified Christ walking amid the Christian communities on earth deals mainly with the present concerns of those churches. These concerns are dealt with in the light of the conditional promises of Jesus to be fulfilled in his future judgement. Likewise the heavenly vision, which now begins, deals with the same tension but with different emphases. Attention is now focused on heaven, the future judgement and salvation (6:12–17; 7:9–17). A more universal dimension, implicit in the selection of seven churches, is stressed. The aim of the writer, as J.P.M. Sweet puts it in his commentary (p 10), is to persuade his audience to "put eternal destiny before apparent security and prosperity in the present." But the aim is not in any way escapist. Rather like that of the early Christian prophets, the aim is concrete and this-wordly, to find guidance and hope for the communities in the present circumstances.

In chapter one a magnificent vision of the risen Jesus was described. Here we begin with a very powerful vision of Yahweh, although the writer does not call it that. In a sense the artist Dürer caught the spirit of the Apocalypse very well in his illustrations. He paints idyllic scenes of a calm German countryside, but overhead he paints bizarre pictures of apocalyptic warfare. What he does is to penetrate beneath the superficial order of society to uncover a Pandora's Box of inner conflicts and warfare at the heart of the people and their world and to project them onto a worldwide horizon. One thinks of Oscar Wilde's warning in his preface to *The Picture of Dorian Gray* that those who would go beneath the surface do so at their peril.

The author's aim of bringing criticism and hope has not changed, even though from chapter four onward he moves much more into his surrealistic world of fantasy. In his opening chapters he has shown that the all-powerful and all-knowing Jesus is not only alive but present to his communities. He is their critic, their final judge and saviour. Next, the camera of the author's mind moves to the heavenly court. There God is pictured as supreme in majesty, even above mighty Rome, and receiving homage from representatives of all creation. He already knows even the future which he has written on a scroll with seven seals. Chapter four focuses on the all-powerful God as creator. The following chapter stresses that he is redeemer. The vision of Jesus the wounded but

conquering Lamb is the climax (5:1–14). A magnificent
representation of this vision is found in Georg Meistermann's
altar piece in the Church of St. Alphonsus, Wurzburg. John
continually refers back to this vision in his work in 7:11;
11:16; 12:5; 14:3; 19:4; 20:11; 21:5. It provides him with the
still point of the universe, the solid core against which the
drama of our lives is played out. Strengthened by such a vision,
a Christian community can face the problems of their lives
with confidence.

The Eternal Worship of God by All his Creation, 4:1–11

The accusation is often made that our vision is too limited
because our God is too small, too unexciting, too uninteresting
in comparison to charismatic figures from pop stars to politi-
cians. John suddenly interrupts our concentration on this
world to invite us to observe a heavenly liturgy, to let our
imagination soar into the presence of the inaccessible Father
and his incredible and indescribable majesty. Only then can
we face the problems of life and see them, as Job learned, from
the proper perspective. Likewise the Danish existentialist
Sören Kierkegaard insisted that each morning before he could
begin his daily round of activities, he felt compelled to satisfy
his own mind with fresh confidence in the existence of God.
According to Paul Minear (New Testament Apocalyptic, p 69)
this vision shows us three aspects of John's perspective. First,
it is his confession of faith in the first commandment "I am the
Lord your God . . . You shall have no other gods before me"
(Ex 20:2f). Secondly, it brings out the wonder and sense of
mystery and personal adventure in a faith that is far richer
than a mere assent to a doctrine. Thirdly, it shows the highest

source of the authority underlying the mission John shared with the seven churches, a mission which demanded a higher priority than the need for health, wealth, or public approval.

"After these things I looked, and behold, an open door ...." The Hebrews tended to imagine the sky as a solid firmament (Gn 1:7–8), and therefore some kind of opening was needed for communication between heaven and earth. To a person familiar with some of the visions of heaven found in the Old Testament (Ez 1:4–26; Dn 7:9–10; Is 6:1–13; 1 Kgs 22:19) this passage in John would present no problems. Such visions often begin with an invitation to look or to enter through the open door (Ac 7:56; Mt 3:16). Several of the phrases such as the trumpet-like voice recall 1:10 (cf Ex 19:16). The description of "what must take place" will be given in 6:1ff. The command to come up was also given to Moses on Mt. Sinai and was used to invite mystics to advance to a higher state. Significantly, early Jewish mysticism is throne mysticism, contemplating not God's real nature but his appearance on his throne. The throne room scene combines images from Solomon's temple (the throne of cherubim, brazen sea, singing, incense, altar of sacrifice) and the synagogue (the scroll) with images of the heavenly court gathered in judgement (2 Chr 3–5; Dn 7:9–14).

Surprisingly, God himself is neither mentioned nor described directly. All is done indirectly and by suggestion, inviting the reader to use the gift of imagination as freely as possible. Thus Yahweh's marvellous transcendence is properly safeguarded and the silence of the throne itself indicates a power and a glory beyond description. In the midst of the scintillating stones, the brilliant rainbow, the elders crowned with gold, the flashing lightning, and peals of thunder, and the flaming torches, there is simply a throne. More than forty times the word "throne" is found in John as if to say that high above the thrones of emperors and political powers with their demands for adoration, there is one important throne with which one must reckon above all. It is not so much a chair as a symbol of God's dignity, power, and transcendent presence. No direct attempt is used to describe the one seated on the throne. Rather, he is like a combination of the three precious stones: the flashing translucent jasper, the fiery red carnelian, and the soft green emerald, which according to Ezek 28:13 were found in paradise. In Ex 28:17–21 these stones are found on the high priest's breastplate representing the first and last tribes of Israel, Benjamin the youngest and Reuben the eldest. The third, the emerald, represented Judah. The stones appear later in the foundations of the new Jerusalem (21:19). The halo or rainbow around the throne recalls Gn 9:13 and Ezek 1:3 although a different Greek word is used there. Ezekiel fell on his face when he saw the rainbow. In Genesis, the rainbow seems to be God's war-bow, and the flashes of lightning his arrows (Ps 7:13; Hab 3:11). The scene describes God's cove-nant with Noah and all humanity and the allusion here is probably a reminder that God is faithful to his ancient promises. Less likely is the suggestion that the rainbow is a sign and a reminder of the wickedness of the earth.

Twenty-four elders in white garments and golden crowns surround the awesome throne, which gives forth flashes of lightning and peals of thunder. These phenomena are typical in Old Testament descriptions of theophanies such as the giving of the law to Moses at Sinai (Ex 19:16; Ezek 1:13; Ps 18:13f; Job 37:2–5). The seven torches of perpetual fire are the seven spirits of God (the Holy Spirit) which oversee the whole universe (1:4). The floor around the throne was like a crystal-clear sea of glass. Typically the author does not say that there *was* a sea, but that it was *like* a sea. Perhaps the image may be drawn from the paved orchestra of a Greek theatre with the living creatures representing the massed chorus. Different interpretations are given. Glass was not very clear in the first century and obviously crystal clear glass would be very unusual. In the Koran's (27) description of the visit of the Queen of Sheba to Solomon, she is described as lifting her skirts because she thought the glass pavement before his throne was one of water. Different interpretations of the heavenly scene are suggested. One is that it represents the sea of humanity in perfect harmony with God without a ripple of trouble on its many waters. G.B. Caird, drawing on the sea monster theme and its mythological background (13:1; 15:2), sees a reference to the cosmic sea of chaos over which God claims authority in creation. Eventually there will be no more sea (21:1). The sea is the reservoir of evil from which the monster arises (13:1). It is the barrier through which the faithful must pass in a new Exodus to the promised land (15:2f). Perhaps the best interpretation is to see the sea simply as a barrier setting apart the awesome inaccessible throne with its thunder and lightning, symbolising the holiness, power, and tremendous majesty of God.

There seem to be four different groups before the throne, the four living creatures at the centre, the twenty four elders, many angels (5:11) and every creature in heaven and on earth (5:13). Each circle has its own hymn of praise in which the others join.

The description of the four creatures is a composite drawn from Ezekiel whose creatures had four different faces and a multitude of eyes arranged on wheels (Ez 1:4–14), and Isaiah (6:2) where the seraphim with six wings are found. The imagery may have been drawn from the Babylonian signs of the zodiac based on the four elements of the cosmos: earth, fire, water, air. The ox, Taurus, was an earth sign; the lion, Leo, a fire sign; Scorpio, the scorpion often drawn with a human face, was a water sign; the eagle, a sign for the air. In later times the four creatures were connected with the four evangelists, generally the man with Matthew, the lion with Mark, the calf with Luke, and the eagle with John. But this is not the original application. The probable symbolism is divine sovereignty over the whole created world in all its variety and ceaseless energy. The phrase "full of eyes" suggests sleepless vigilance and secret ceaseless energy. Being "full of eyes" symbolises a nature which never rests but is constantly praising God. The function of the four creatures who are mentioned fourteen times in the book is to act as masters of ceremonies or choirmasters leading all the public worship in heaven in constantly praising God and proclaiming his holiness — "hallowed be thy name." By symbolising the cosmos they remind us that God is not aloof in a remote heaven but that he is at the heart of our universe, the ground of our being, to quote a modern phrase.

Some thirteen different views have been suggested as to the identity of the twenty-four elders who are mentioned some twelve times in the book. These interpretations range from the twenty-four stars in the heavens or judges ruling the universe to a simple symbolic presentation of fullness or totality. The thrones and white garments seem to indicate that they are kingly priests sharing in God's rule. R.H. Charles concludes that the elders are angels or heavenly representatives of all the faithful in their priestly and royal roles. The picture is that of an oriental king's throne room surrounded by twenty-four vassal kings giving homage. According to A. Feuillet, these elders are not angels but human beings, an interpretation based on the analogy of Hebrews 11:2ff, which has the same term (elders). Elders symbolize the Old Testament saints whom the Christians considered to be their ancestors in the faith. They are numbered twenty-four because, according to the Book of Chronicles (1 Chr 24:3–19; 25:6–31), this was the basic number for the organization of the temple cult.

The function of the four creatures' ceaseless doxology is to proclaim the essential nature of God, his holiness, power, and eternity, the last two having been mentioned already in 1:4,8. In contrast, the following hymn of the elders celebrates the glory of God in his works. In Hebrew the repetition of a word adds emphasis but the rare threefold repetition "Holy, Holy," the trisagion as it is called, designates the superlative. This trisagion became a liturgical expression in both Jewish and Christian liturgies. It is a confession of faith: God alone, not Caesar, is the holiest, most powerful and everlasting one. For the Hebrews the holiness of Yahweh is seen in his speech, his acts, his power, and his character. It is not primarily an ethical attribute, but it becomes ethical or moral when Yahweh is compared with sinful people. The Hebrews experienced Yahweh's holiness in a special way in the cult. The holy was defined by Rudolf Otto as the "wholly other," the divine attribute which combines the fearful and the fascinating. For a person to be holy means to be set apart and dedicated to the one holy Yahweh. In the targums on the Isaian trisagion each holy was developed into a poetic verse:

Holy in the highest heavens, the house of his presence;
Holy on earth, the work of his might, Holy for endless ages.

But Isaiah's trisagion continues to say that "the whole earth is full of his glory," a point which would not have suited John's view of the alienated creation.

In recent times of liturgical renewal, many critics point out that what is missing is Mystery, the experience of the holy. John would like the words of the second paragraph of the Vatican II Constitution on the Sacred Liturgy :

Liturgy is the outstanding means by which the faithful can express in their lives and manifest to others the mystery of Christ and the real nature of the Church.

Thus the four living creatures gave glory, honour, and thanks to the eternal one who sits on the throne. Glory signifies importance, the essential inner value of a person, which demands respect from others. Honour signifies esteem or value. Thanks is what is due to God because of his incredible, creative love. Their song leads in turn to a second song from the elders. There are in all five brief hymns in chapters 4 and 5 with a gradually increasing choir, the first two addressed to God, the following two to the Lamb, and the fifth to both (5:13). Many popular hymn writers have received their inspiration from these brief hymns.

The elders take their cue from the living creatures and burst into an acclamation of God's worthiness "because of your will they continually exist and have come into being." Their worship involves three acts: prostration before the throne, casting their crowns before the throne, and singing. According to the Roman historian, Tacitus, the Parthian king Tiridates placed his crown before the image of the emperor Nero in order to do him homage. Emperor Diocletian was acclaimed as "Lord and God" and greeted with the cry "worthy are you" in his triumphal entry. In the "worthy" hymn, which is a choral response to the first doxology, "power" replaces "thanks."

The Scroll and the Lamb, 5:1–14

With his X-ray vision the author continues to pierce behind the seeming reality of things to show that there is more to life than what meets the eye. Jesus, though crucified, is at the heart of the universe and is the real controller of all destinies and lives. The faithful may appear powerless, but the risen Jesus is the king of kings and the lord of the lords of the earth. Our writer is full of surprises and a master of suspenseful delay. Wonderful though the glorious vision of chapter 4 is, with its all-embracing doxology, taken by itself it simply does not ring true to the reality of sinful, suffering humanity. To quote Plato, the vision does not save the phenomena. John's answer is the addition of chapter 5 with its emphasis on the mysterious scroll and the key event of the slaughter of the Lamb. Paul Minear (*New Testament Apocalyptic*, p 72) cites two thought-provoking quotations to illustrate how the "other world" of the throne is made inseparable from our world of the Cross. He first quotes the Jewish scholar Martin Buber's explanation as to why he cannot accept Jesus as Messiah.

Either one takes the condition of the world seriously or one does not. If one does, then its transformation has clearly not occurred and the Christian claim to have found in Jesus of Nazareth the Messiah of God cannot be honored.

His second quotation comes from Paul W. Meyer.

Only Christians have a Good Friday. Only they recall in text and liturgy a public historical event that once made, and still makes, a mockery of their most central claim, and yet (they) return to it as their most central truth: the coming of the Messiah in an unredeemed world.

Suddenly and surprisingly the author focuses on the right hand of the one sitting on the throne and on the scroll which was held there. The point of the right hand is clearly anthropomorphic and symbolic of God's power. In the ancient world books were the possession of the rich few, and to many, who saw them only from a distance, they had a mysterious air about them. One familiar with the Old Testament would quickly recall the scene in Ezekiel 2:9–3:1 where the prophet eats the scroll unrolled before him:

It was covered with writing front and back, and written on it was: lamentation and wailing and woe!

John's description differs in that the scroll is sealed, a point that recalls the instruction to Daniel to "keep secret the message and seal the book until the end time; many shall fall away and evil shall increase" (Dn 12:4). Much discussion has centred on how to describe the actual scroll with its seven seals. In the East a clay document sometimes had its message repeated on the other side, and a protective cover was added to guard against falsification. The same process was occasionally adopted when papyrus was used. The seven seals show the great importance of the message. Perhaps the book was in a flat codex form because a scroll could be opened and read only after all the seals were broken. The following chapters show that the breaking of a seal meant that a further part of the message could be read. Ancient Roman wills or testaments were sealed with six seals, giving rise to the suggestion that the scroll is God's testament.

The content and nature of the scroll is somewhat enigmatic, not surprisingly, several interpretations have been offered. One popular interpretation is that it involves the Old Testament, of which the true meaning is hidden until the coming of Christ (Lk 4:21; 2 Cor 3:14). But how is Christ's victory through death the necessary qualification? Another less likely view is that the scroll is the book of life (3:5) revealing the names of the redeemed, but this revelation does not take place. A third view is that it is a record of events soon to take place. However, John is writing some 60 years after the death of Jesus, and there seems to be no reason for this delay in opening the seal. Any explanation should obviously be based on the subsequent chapters of the book as we have it. These describe God's redemptive plan for salvation, his future involvement in history culminating in the parousia, a plan already foreshadowed in the Old Testament.

The loud proclamation of the mighty angel: "Who is worthy to open the scroll and to break its seals?" which plays on the word "worthy" of the previous hymn, is in reality a critique of contemporary apocalyptic interpretations. No one but Christ can unlock the hidden purposes and plan of the mysterious Yahweh for creation. Jesus is not only the succes-

sor of the partial revelations found in Ezekiel and Daniel but
he is the final revelation of God's activity in human history.
The answer to the angel's question,

> No one has the power,
> no one . . . in the heavens,
> no one on the earth,
> no one under the earth,

is given a triadic dirge form. The verb "klaio," used of John's
wailing, is also used for those who mourn the death of Lazarus
(Jn 11:33) in contrast to the other verb used of Jesus' own
tears (Jn 11:35). But an anonymous elder bids John "stop
crying." Two familiar Old Testament messianic titles, "the
Lion of the tribe of Judah" and "the root of David" are used to
describe the one who has conquered (2:7). They are linked
together only here and in the Qumran literature. The lion is
the animal most often mentioned in the Bible. It was used of
God (Is 31:4), Israel (Num 23:24), Saul, and Jonathan (2 Sm
1:23). Lions were depicted on the throne of Solomon (1 Kgs
10:19–20). The symbolism was one of majestic strength,
courage, menace, even of intellectual excellence. The actual
phrase "the Lion of the tribe of Judah" is found only here in
the Bible, but there is an obvious allusion to Genesis where, in
Jacob's last blessing to his sons, Judah is described as a lion's
whelp and there is a promise that "the sceptre shall never
depart from Judah" (Gn 49:10). In 4 Ezra 11:36–46, a Jewish
apocalypse roughly contemporary with John, the lion appears
to pronounce doom against the fourth imperial beast, the
Roman eagle. Similarly, in John the opening of the scroll spells
doom for the imperial power of Rome.

Likewise the expression "The Root of David" is not found
in the Old Testament, but there are references to the root of
Jesse, David's father (Is 11:1; Sir 47:22). According to Isaiah
the Spirit of the Lord will rest upon "the root." He will strike
the ruthless and slay the wicked and be a "signal for the
nations whom the Gentiles will seek out."

John looks for this Lion and paradoxically he sees "a Lamb
standing as if slain." The conquest through death, through
what we call the paschal mystery (5:6-14; Rom 5:18), is not
what one would expect from a conventional Davidic warrior.
This emphasis on sacrifical death recalls the Old Testament
passover lamb and the Suffering Servant of Isaiah (Ex 12:5f; Is
53:7). In the Jewish Apocalypse, Enoch the Lamb grows into a
great horned ram to conquer the hostile beasts which attack
God's people. Thus the image is paradoxical.

The lamb has seven horns and seven eyes which seem to
symbolise total control and omniscience in the whole universe. The presence of the lamb shows that at the heart or
centre of God and his designs, as it were, stands "a little
Lamb." A different Greek word is used for Christ elsewhere in
the New Testament but the vision seems to be the same. The
Lamb is a conqueror by mounting on the throne of the cross
(Jn 1:29; Ac 8:32; 1 P 1:19). The symbol of the Lamb, a word
used twenty-nine times, dominates John's thinking in the rest
of the book. The Lamb is adored (v 8), has bought people by
his blood and made them a kingdom and priests (5:9f), makes
kings hide from his anger (6:16), is the saviour, leader and
shepherd of others (7:10,17), is judge (13:8), stands on Mt.
Sion (14: Sion (14:1–5), is victorious in war (17:14), is a
temple (21:22), and shares God's throne (22:1). The commentator J.P. Love in the *Layman's Bible Commentary* remarks:

None but an inspired composer of heavenly vision would ever have thought of it. When earth-bound men want symbols of power they conjure up mighty beasts and birds of prey. Russia elevates the bear, Britain the lion, France the tiger, the United States the spread eagle — all of them ravenous. It is only the Kingdom of Heaven that would dare to use as its symbol of might, not the Lion for which John was looking but the helpless Lamb, and at that a slain Lamb.

Dramatically the Lamb "came and took" the scroll. This action leads to three great outbursts of praise, in ever widening circles, from the four living creatures and the elders, from many angels and from every creature. The first group perform a threefold act of worship by prostration, prayers and the singing of a new song. They prostrate themselves in worship before the Lamb as they had earlier done to God (4:10), thus placing both on the same level. Each has a lyre or zither, the type of harp then used in worship (14:2; Ps 33:2). Also they have golden bowls full of incense which symbolise the prayers of the saints, a symbolism also found in Psalm 141:2. The liturgical description then involves the whole person — sight, sound, movement, smell.

The word "saints" does not signify Christians of heroic virtue but rather is the common New Testament word for dedicated Christians (11:18; 2 Cor 1:1; Phil 1:1). Thus John assures his community that, although they may seem to be of little power or value on earth, their petitions are presented to the risen Christ in his glory (8:3ff). The third act of worship is to sing a new "ode," the New Testament word for a sacred song. Frequently the biblical text bursts into song upon Yahweh's mighty interventions. New songs are described in the Bible when new unprecedented acts of God's mercy are celebrated in praise (14:3; Ps 33:3; 96:1). Like a modern commercial, John continually stresses the theme of newness — name, Jerusalem, heaven and earth, all things. The three hymns celebrate the opening of the scroll by the Lamb. The first two praise the Lamb while the third also celebrates the one on the throne. The singers increase from twenty-eight in the first to every creature in the universe in the third.

The new song acclaiming Christ's worthiness, qualifications ("axios" means capable of, fit, equal to, deserving, comparable) gives three reasons: you were slain, you purchased for God by your blood people from every tribe, you have made them a priestly kingdom for our God and they shall reign on earth. The word "worthy" seems to have been borrowed from secular usage, as it does not seem to have been used in religious texts.

The verb "slain" refers to the victorious death of Jesus. It was no mythological or accidental death but real and deliberate. The word used suggests a violent death of a martyr, for it is never used of a sacrificial death in the New Testament. The centrality of the crucifixion is continually stressed by John. There may be an allusion to the Paschal Lamb and the Exodus which were used to interpret Christ's violent death (1 Cor 5:7; 1 Pt 1:18). The sacrifice of lambs in the temple was also seen as a memorial of the binding of Isaac for sacrifice, which was believed to have a permanent redemptive effect on the Israelites. Thus the Maccabee martyrs were warned to remember Isaac who surrendered himself in sacrifice (4 Mac 13:12).

Secondly, the Lamb is worthy because he is God's purchasing agent with his blood. The verb "redeem" simply means "purchase." The aim of the purchase is that people may belong to God (1 Cor 6:19f). The price is the blood of Jesus. The image seems to be the Exodus liberation of the slaves and the practice in society of buying back prisoners of war (Ex 19:6). But the use of the metaphor is limited here because no one in particular is mentioned as receiving the price. The symbolism of blood was very important in the biblical tradition. The blood of the Paschal Lamb smeared on the doorposts saved the Hebrews from losing their first-born (Ex 12:7ff). Blood was also believed to cleanse from sin. On the Day of Atonement the high priest sprinkled blood in a ritual ceremony to remind the people that Yahweh was a forgiving God who wished to remove guilt and sin and to effect a life-giving reconciliation with his people. Blood had sealed the covenant at Sinai (Ex 24:3–8).

But the symbolism was not only salvific. It seems that, unique among their neighbours, the Hebrews linked blood with life and the sacred and therefore with Yahweh the God of life (Gn 9:4; Lev 17:11). Thus the new song in the Apocalypse is a song of thanksgiving for life. When the missionary bishop Hannington was about to be martyred in Africa he is reported to have sent the king this message: "Go and tell king Mwanga that I have purchased the road to Uganda with my blood."

Thirdly, the universal scope of Christ's worthy victory is indicated by four words which John likes to join together: "people of every tribe, language, people, and nation" (Dn 3:4). This priestly kingdom is not just a future hope but a present gift (1:6). Surprisingly, it is not so much God or Christ but the Christians who are to reign. This statement must have seemed incredible to many. As a church historian once pointed out, in the fierce contest between the Church and the empire, only one side was armed and that was the side which lost.

Next John sees a new chorus of "myriads of myriads and thousands of thousands" of angels (Dn 7:10). These cry out, like the sound of a mighty gong, with a seven-fold acclamation which recalls David's last prayer (1 Chr 29:11–13).Surprisingly, one commentator suggests that the angels cannot sing the new song because they have not fallen and have no need to be redeemed. Further there is nothing in the Bible which says that angels sing at all! The angels repeat three of the elders' terms of praise — power, honour, and glory (4:11). They add riches, wisdom, strength, and praise to make a total of seven, symbolising the fullness of their praise. The last three describe the attitude of people to Jesus while the first four describe Jesus' qualities. Almost all of these qualities are applied to Christ elsewhere in the New Testament: power (1 Cor 1:24); riches (2 Cor 8:9); wisdom (1 Cor 1:24); strength (Eph 6:10); honour (Heb 2:9); glory (Jn 1:14), praise or blessing (Mk 11:9f). A surprising one perhaps is "riches." Paul says Christ, who was rich, became poor and made us rich.

The third and final circle of praise comes from every creature including the sea creatures (5:3). In contrast to the doxology of 4:8, this new song specifically mentions the worship of the Lamb who is associated with God himself in what scholars call the "high christology" (3:21). Three of the previous acclamations are repeated — praise, honour, glory — and dominion or sovereignty is added. The chapter concludes with a great Amen as the elders fall down in worship.

One can easily visualise the whole scene from the doorway of a medieval cathedral. During a solemn celebration the bishop presides from his throne in the sanctuary with its wide expanse of shining marble. He is surrounded by the elders, priests and deacons. The choir is filled with a variety of musicians and singers while the nave is filled with the people. At key moments the whole church is filled with sweet smelling incense. The author's purpose is not so much to describe the liturgy of heaven as to give hope and a sense of victory to the people in the struggle which lies ahead.

2). THE OPENING OF THE SIX SEALS, 6:1–7:17

The worthiness of the Lamb has been celebrated in heaven and his final victory predicted. Now the consequences on earth of his opening the seven seals are described. This vision of the seals, like the following cycle of the seven trumpets, describes the whole story of the Christian Church moving through persecution to judgement and final triumph. The opening of the first six seals is placed between the anticipated victory of the Lamb in chapter 5 and the triumph of the saints in chapter 7. With the opening of the first four the celebrated Four Horsemen of the Apocalypse are set loose to bring disasters upon the whole world. When the fifth is opened, there is a vision of the souls of the slain Christians asking how long God will delay his judgement. Then, with the opening of the sixth seal, further disasters take place.

Scholars have long debated the meaning of the first four seals (in particular). Do they, from John's vantage point, refer to the past, the present, or the future? Do they deal with the events which occur throughout the life of the Church? Or do they run in sequence? Or are they a description of the final drama or of the events leading up to it? The position taken here is that at least the first four should not be taken as detailed predictions of events destined to take place one after another. Rather, each describes one aspect of a future time of woe, of the birthpangs of the new creation. The present state, as the seven letters show, is not one of intense suffering and disaster. The aim of the author is not so much to provide information about the future as to challenge, to shock his community into facing up to its present responsibilities as Christians giving witness to their risen Lord. This he does by giving a poetic, highly symbolic and even hyperbolic vision of the future. Note how he is careful to insist that, no matter what disaster strikes, God is in control of universe. The Lamb will ultimately conquer (17:14). Yet it is the same Lamb who opens the seals to set off the disasters and permits their testing and suffering. But he does not ascribe all the disasters to the direct vindictive will of God. The repeated phrase "it was given" suggests the tolerance and permission of God as he allows the evil of the world to run its course. Suffering is part of his providence. John would agree with the Pauline view that God works all unto good. In fact his hymns seem to suggest that ultimately every creature will praise God.

For a better understanding of this whole section a preliminary reading of some other biblical texts is of great help. A good place to begin is the prophecy of sevenfold doom repeated four times in Leviticus 26:

> I will increase the chastisement for your sins sevenfold to break your haughty confidence (Lv 26:18ff).

Next one could read the fantastic world of Ezekiel, the prophet of the Exile. He sees himself as a watchman warning Israel about its unfounded hopes for a reversal of its fortunes. He falls into a cataleptic stupor for seven days and then dramatically enacts one sign after another to compel his people to pay attention. He makes a clay brick to resemble Jerusalem and then proceeds to simulate a siege of the city. He lies for 150 days on his right side and 40 days on his left while eating only the skimpy and defiled rations of a starving people to highlight the coming exile. Then in chapter 5 he cuts off his hair and disposes of it in separate lots to demonstrate the fate which lies in wait for Jerusalem's inhabitants. In chapter 5:12–17 he has God himself pronounce a terrible curse bringing on the four plagues of Leviticus 26 — a third of the people will be killed by plague and hunger, a third by war, and the rest carried to exile. It is not difficult to recognise the influence of Ezekiel 6:7,8 of John's Apocalypse.

Another clear influence on our author is found in the visions of the late sixth century prophet, Zechariah, in his chapters 1 and 6 (see further Hab 3:4–15; Jer 15:2). In both of these texts, four horses of various colours are sent to patrol the earth and to judge the enemies of God's people. In the second text of Zechariah more than four horses are involved. Three of the colours, red, black, and white, correspond to those in John, but the symbolism is different. John, typically, has his own original touch. The four horsemen of the Apocalypse stand for plagues and disasters to come on the earth. What is particularly different from the Jewish apocalypses is the emphasis on the place of the Christian faithful, the martyrs and the redeemed.

This leads us to a final passage, the so-called Little Apocalypse of Mark 13:7–9,24–5, and its parallels in Matthew 24 and Luke 21. R.H.Charles pointed out that the seven judgements in John are to be found in the Lord's eschatological discourse. In Luke they are found in the same order, except that John typically places the earthquake last as the immediate forerunner of the consummation. The correspondence to the "beginning of birth pangs" in Jesus' discourse on Mt. Olivet is too obvious to be ignored. There, war is followed by international conflict, earthquakes, famine, and heavenly signs not unlike John's more extended version of the cavalry charge of the horses.

(i) The White Horse of Conquest, 6:1–2

As the Lamb opens the first seal a thunderous voice, from one of the living creatures, speaks the simple but urgent command "come."

The identity of the white horse with its rider and his bow have been much disputed. The word for white can also mean gray as in Zechariah's description of the horse (Zech 1:8) or even pink or reddish white. Irenaeus and many after him interpret the rider on the white horse to be the victorious Christ spreading his gospel to the whole earth before the end (Mk 13:10). White is normally associated with Christ and his justice in the Apocalypse. Towards the end of the book, in 19:11–16, there is a portrayal of Christ riding a white horse and being called "Faithful and True" and "Word of God," with justice as "his standard in waging war." But the latter may be in direct contrast to the first rider (a false Christ!) who conquers with his bow. The bow was not a normal Roman weapon but was the weapon of the expansionist Babylonians (Jer 51:56) and the Parthians who defeated the Romans in a battle in A.D. 62. Not surprisingly the Romans feared an invasion from the mysterious Parthians. Some of the peoples in the eastern Mediterranean, including quite a few Jews and quite possibly John himself, hoped that the Parthians would conquer the Roman Empire and its satanic power (9:13–21). Thus it seems best to take the first seal as forming a unity with the following three. They symbolize the disasters which conquering empires brought and which were quite familiar to John's audience.

(ii) The Red Horse of Civil War, 6:3–4

"Fiery Red" symbolizes bloodshed and slaughter (2 Kgs 3:22f). The rider receives the power "to take peace from the earth by alluring men to slaughter one another," a contrast to the gift of God's peace at the beginning of the book (1:4). While the first seal speaks of wars of conquest, John seems to be alluding to some of the internal wars and mass murders with which his audience was quite familiar. One estimate shows that between 67 and 37 B.C. some 100,000 people were killed in Palestine while during the revolt in Britain in A.D. 61 under Queen Boadicea some 150,000 were killed. Other wars in Germany, Armenia and Parthia from A.D. 41-A.D.54 are recorded. The period after Nero's death in A.D. 69 saw three different emperors in quick succession and civil wars that shook the empire to its roots. Perhaps John also has in mind the death of Antipas (2:13) or the persecution under Nero and Domitian.

(iii) The Black Horse of Famine, 6:5–6

The rider of the rather ominous black horse is described as holding a pair of scales or a balance in his hand. The symbolism is not of justice (Prov 16:11; Ezek 45:10) but refers to the weighing of bread in time of famine which naturally would follow the civil wars of the previous seal. The allusion is to Ezekiel's prediction before the siege of Jerusalem:

> Son of man, I am breaking the staff of bread in Jerusalem. They shall eat bread which they have weighed out anxiously, and they shall drink water which they have measured out fearfully (Ezek 4:16; Lv 26:26).

In the Roman world famines were not infrequent because so many people lived at survival level.

A mysterious voice or rather "as it were a voice" from among the living creatures gives an economic explanation: a day's wage (a denarius) for a quart of wheat or three quarts of barley but "do not injure the oil and the wine." A quart of wheat was a solider's ration for a day according to military records. Barley was mixed in by the poor — three quarts would be a poor family's food for a day. In Cicero's day, a day's wages would have purchased 12 quarts of wheat and 24 of barley. The implications are a scarcity of the staple food bread but not a famine of disastrous dimensions. Some of the Fathers suggest that the oil and wine are preserved because of their importance for the liturgy. But there seems to be no basis in the text for this view. If the oil and wine are seen as luxuries then the picture is one of the rich eating plenty and the poor barely surviving. However it seems more obvious that oil and wine were also staple foods. If so, the conclusion of the third seal is a partial famine.

(iv) The Pale Horse of Death, 6:7–8

From the Greek word for pale (yellow, green, ashen or corpse-coloured) comes the English word chlorine. The rider Death, who naturally follows the famine of the third seal, has no emblem. Close behind is Hades, the ruler of the underworld. Later we will be told that the followers of the Lamb have nothing to fear because Hades and Death are thrown into the lake of fire (20:14). The phrase "power was given" reminds the Christian communities that even now Death and Hades are under the control of God and his Lamb. The power of death is limited to a quarter of the population of the earth. Later there is an intensification as the trumpets destroy a third (8:7ff) and the bowls complete the destruction (16:1ff). The four agents of death, the sword, famine, plague, and wild beasts, are the four cruel punishments described by Ezekiel (14:21).

According to the commentator Swete, the first four seals describe John's analysis of the Roman Empire — "outwardly victorious and eager for fresh conquests, yet full of the elements of unrest, danger, and misery; war, scarcity, pestilence, mortality in all its forms!" This is a series of pictures which repeats itself in history. Militarism and the lust of conquest are among the forces set loose by Christ to prepare for his coming and the final revelation of the sealed scroll.

(v) The Fifth Seal, The Martyrs, 6:9–11

In the fifth seal the living creatures, the horsemen and their riders roaming the earth, take no part. Instead John sees "under the altar the spirits of those who had been martyred because of the witness they bore to the word of God." The general atmosphere of the previous throne scene suggests a temple vision. Now we have the first reference to an altar. The other altar in the Apocalypse can be interpreted as the altar of incense near the Holy of Holies (8:3; 11:1). The reference to the altar may indicate that martyrdom was an act of prayer or even of sacrifice. But the more natural way of describing a sacrifice would be "on," not "under," the altar. The idea of people buried under the altar is a Jewish concept. Further, in Jewish tradition the death of a martyr was seen as a vicarious sacrifice for the people, one that restrains God's wrath and brings about reconciliation (2 Mc 7:37). John's martyrs may include both the Old Testament martyrs and those of the first century (13:15; 18:24; 20:4; Mk 13:9–13; Mt 23:32–36).

The martyrs' address to God as "master" and "true" is paralleled by the words which the historian Josephus puts in the mouth of Eleazar the zealot commander at Masada:

> We have resolved for a long time to be subject neither to the Romans nor to anyone else, but to God alone, for he alone is the true and just master of men (Wars 7.323).

The loud cry for justice, which recalls the appeal of Abel's blood and the frequent "how long" phrase in the Old Testament, has disturbed many comfortable Christians who have little or no experience of persecution (Gn 4:10; Ps 6:3; 79:5; Is 6:11; Jer 47:6; Dn 12:6; Zech 1:12). At first sight it seems to contrast sharply with the Lucan prayers for forgiveness by Jesus himself and by Stephen (Lk 23:34; Ac 7:60). But, on reflection, an attitude of forgiveness and longing for God's justice instead of the harsh reality, for his will to be done on earth, are not incompatible, as the Our Father shows. John's prayer is the Matthaean beatitude "Blessed are those who hunger and thirst for justice." It follows in the long line of courageous questioning in the Bible, going back at least to Habakkuk. Habakkuk seems to have been the first Jewish Literature to question God's silence and his ways of governing the world. The criticism of Job's comforters in the Book of Job shows that such people are only defending their own prejudiced view of the holiness which God requires. John's view is not unlike Paul's advice in Romans 12:19 —

Beloved, do not avenge yourselves; leave that to God's wrath, for it is written "Vengeance is mine; I will repay," says the Lord.

John's community may not have had much actual experience of martyrdom but he is dramatically trying to convince them of its value.

God's reply to the martyr's prayer is threefold: each was given a long white robe, advice to rest for a little while longer, and the reason for the delay: that the quota of their fellow servants and brothers to be slain was not yet filled up. The white robe symbolises victory (3:4) and justification (19:8). The notion of waiting for a little while longer is found in 4 Ezra 4:33–37. There the souls of the just ask how long they must remain in their chambers. The archangel Jeremiel answers that they must wait until the number of the just is fulfilled. But this passage in John must not be interpreted as if a cruel God needs so many to die. Rather the writer is insisting that he does not understand the full extent of the plan of God. However, his intention is to encourage. He is insisting that there is a limit to the seemingly endless suffering of God's people. The latter is composed of martyrs and non-martyrs or fellow servants like John himself. G.B. Caird speculates that God's victories come through the faithfulness of the just.

(vi) The Sixth Seal, 6:12–17

In sharp contrast to the previous seal with its prayer of the martyrs, we now are given a picture of the wrath of the Lamb over a hostile world. In traditional Jewish thinking cosmic catastrophe is a result of human sin. The catastrophe painted here in hyperbolic terms draws on the Old Testament prophets and in particular on the apocalyptic discourses which Jesus pronounces towards the end of the synoptic gospels (Mk 13:4-19). Seven phenomena of nature are described: the earthquake, the darkening of the sun, the moon becoming like blood, the stars falling, the rolling up of the heavens, the removal of mountains and islands. The order of destruction is roughly the same as the order of creation in Genesis, leading to the people's hiding from the presence of God just as Adam and Eve had done (Gn 3:8).

The picture is symbolic — the number seven signifies totality of completeness. No enemy of the Lamb can escape his wrath. There is no place left to hide. Seven social classes are mentioned showing that, no matter what one's position, there is no escape for those who refuse to repent: kings, great people, the strong, the generals, the rich, the slaves, the free. The cry of people for the mountains and rocks to fall on them and hide them is found in the judgement predictions of Is 2:19ff and Hos 10:8. Likewise Jesus predicted that the inhabitants of Jerusalem would cry out to escape God's judgement (Lk 23:30). Thus, the sixth seal differs from the previous seals and brings them to a climax with its revelation of a personal judgement and punishment in contrast to their emphasis on earthly punishments of a political and social nature.

The chapter ends with the ominous question "Who can stand?" before the Lamb's wrath (Nah 1:6; Mal 3:2). The inspiring chapter 7 begins with a vision of four angels standing with which John wishes to reassure his community. The wrath of God and the Lamb will be a continuous theme in the trumpet and bowl scenes. For Paul, this "wrath" is not just an eschatological judgement but also a present reality (Rom 1:18ff; 2:5). Many people are disturbed by the paradoxical notion of the wrath of the (gentle!) Lamb. Anger describes an essential aspect of God's mysterious reality. In the Old Testament it is often the equivalent of what justice is in modern theological reflection about God. The Old Testament however normally rejects the ancient Mesopotamian idea of a capricious god irrationally producing catastrophes. Yahweh's anger is connected with human sin and associated with his saving covenant, his holiness, his judgements. God is no sponge God. A misconception which often arises is to associate anger primarily with the Old Testament God and love with the New Testament Jesus. This is based on the fact that only once in the words of Jesus is the wrath of God mentioned (Lk 21:23). On the contrary the gospel picture is that Jesus showed anger at the heartlessness of the Pharisees (Mk 3:5) and the unbelief of the crowd (Mt 17:7). Anger is associated with Jesus the judge (Mt 7:23; 24:51; Lk 12:46).

An interesting aspect of the debate concerning the meaning of the wrath of God in Paul (Rom 1:18ff; 2:5) is the view of C.H. Dodd that there is a surprising reserve in Paul's language. He never uses the verb, "to be angry," with God as its subject. The expression "the wrath" is often used by him but only three times are the words "of God" added and only once in an undisputed letter (Rom 1:18; Col 3:6; Eph 5:6). Dodd concludes that the biblical writers when speaking of wrath and judgement are thinking of actual or expected events, which are seen as the inevitable results of sin. On the contrary, in speaking of love and mercy they envisage mainly the personal relationship between God and his people. But Dodd's view has been shown to be too one-sided. A Jew would never imagine God working like a thermostat through abstract, impersonal, automatic laws. God is essentially personal and caring. While neither capricious nor irrational, God obviously has the deep personal abhorrence of the holy one who cares in the midst of cruelty and all forms of injustice. He consistently and responsibly opposes evil in all its forms and will condemn it in the end.

Who can Stand?, 7:1–17

Chapter 7, which includes two visions and a long explanation (7:13–17), provides an interlude before the opening of the seventh seal. The tone changes as the author switches from his emphasis on the dreadful final judgement to focus on the martyrs mentioned briefly at the opening of the fifth seal. His aim is to describe the security of God's people amid the destruction to come. This vision, which we read in the liturgy of the Feast of All Saints, is an anticipation of the vision of the end presented at the conclusion of the book (21:3–4). In fact, the author could easily have ended his work here. Two main themes are developed in this chapter: God's restraining hand over the destructive forces of the world until the elect are sealed; and the final reunion of the faithful with the Lamb in heaven, which provides a fitting climax to the vision of heaven.

The first vision (7:1–8) opens with a description of God restraining the evil of the world. God's four angels hold back the four winds of the earth from blowing on the land, sea or trees. All is under God's control. The four winds are clearly destructive powers — in Dn 7:2 the four winds stir up the great sea from which emerge the four destructive beasts; and in Jer 49:36 the four winds from the four ends of heaven will break the might of Elam and scatter the people. The phrase "the four corners of the earth" indicates an ancient understanding of the earth as a flat square. The fact that nothing

further is said about these winds leads to the conclusion that
the four winds are a new symbol for the four horsemen and for
the disasters which will occur under the trumpets and bowls
(8:2ff). Anyone familiar with the desert winds in the Near
East can appreciate the symbolism of wind as a destructive
force. The natural question is the fate of the believer amid the
dreadful catastrophes which are expected.

In answer, a fifth angel appears from "the rising of the sun"
— the east was the source of glory, light, healing, and hope
(Ezek 43:2; Mal 4:2). He holds the seal of the living God (Dn
6:17; Gn 41:42). The idea of the seal suggests ownership,
belonging, and even protection from the wrath of the Lamb. In
Ezek 9:4 a divine messenger with an ink-horn is told to go
through the city of Jerusalem to mark an X on the foreheads of
those who mourn the abominations of Jerusalem. Others are
sent then to strike everybody without pity except those
marked with an X. Other Old Testament allusions would be
the blood on the doorposts of Egypt (Ex 12:23) and the sealing
of the chosen ones in Is 44:5 where names such as "I am the
Lord's" are written on the hand. Elsewhere in the New
Testament the sealing of the chosen is referred to the presence
of the Holy Spirit (2 Cor 1:22; Eph 1:13). In the second
century the notion of the seal is attached to the washing at
Baptism.

In 9:4 the demonic locusts are commanded to harm only
those who do not have the seal of God on their foreheads.
What protection then is involved if the faithful can suffer and
even be beheaded? (20:4). According to Charles, the servants
of God are protected from demonic forces but do not escape
from physical harm from the plagues, the Antichrist, or even
from the danger of spiritual apostasy. They will be able to

come out of the great tribulation (v 14) and escape from the wrath of the Lamb because now they are God's special possession.

Then John hears the number and identity of the sealed —144,000 from all the tribes of Israel. The main problem in this chapter is to identify the 144,000 and to understand their relationship to the great multitude from all the nations mentioned in v 9. A glance at the detailed commentaries shows considerable divergence of opinion as to whether the references to the twelve tribes are symbolic, representative, or literal. Only a brief overview can be given here.

At first sight the first group of 144,000 servants are Jewish Christians distinct from the second group of unnumbered Gentile Christians. The Jewish emphasis, the naming of the twelve tribes in the first part, and the emphasis on the origin of the multitude from all nations support this argument. In 14:1–5 the 144,000 appear with the Lamb on Mt. Sion and seem to be a special group among the faithful. St. Augustine in his *City of God* (20:29) wrote that Christians teach that, before the judgement, the great and mighty prophet Elijah would convert the Jews to Christ. However, a majority of more recent scholars suggest that both groups are the same people distinguished only by their location. The number 144,000, composed of the square of twelve (the number of Israel) and the square of ten (the number of perfection), is symbolic of an innumerable multitude and refers to the Christians living on earth. The second multitude, however, are in heaven and have endured and survived through the great tribulation. John does not elsewhere make a distinction between Gentile and Jewish Christians. Rather, he tends to equate the Christian with the true Israel (2:9).

The order of the twelve tribes differs from every other order that we have. However, the twenty lists in the Old Testament have eighteen different orders ranging from ten to thirteen and one should be careful in attributing any importance to the specific order found here. Yet it seems likely that Judah is put first because Christ is the Lion of Judah (5:5). Dan is omitted because of its association with idolatry or because, as Irenaeus and Hippolytus point out, the Antichrist was expected from the tribe of Dan. Ephraim, likewise omitted, was associated with idolatry. Manasseh, although included in Joseph, is added to make up the twelve. The twelve tribes were no longer a historical reality when John was writing. The ten which made up the northern kingdom of Israel had virtually disappeared several centuries before to become absorbed among the nations. According to some traditions they were in hiding to return before the day of Yahweh. A Christian book like the Epistle of James can however call the Christians dispersed throughout the Roman Empire "the twelve tribes in the dispersion" (Jam 1:1; 1 Pt 1:1).

In his second vision (7:9–17) John paints an unforgettable picture of a vast multitude from every nation. Clad in white robes (3:5) with palms in their hands they stand before the heavenly throne, celebrating the salvation which belongs to God and the Lamb. According to Jn 12:13 Jesus' triumphal entry into Jerusalem was celebrated with palm branches, the symbol of joyful victory. The theme of the song in chapter 5 was worthiness, but here it is the salvation which belongs to God and the Lamb. Again seven adjectives of praise are used. The same word for salvation, "soteria," recurs in 12:10 and 19:1 for the final manifestation of God's kingdom and power. In Luke 2:30 it is used for the messianic salvation. Roman emperors used the term "saviour" to describe the peace and well-being that they provided to the world. Salvation, for John, means standing before God's throne, enjoying his presence and serving him day and night (v 15).

In a literary device, similar to Old Testament apocalyptic passages (Zech 4;13), an interpreting angel asks two questions about the identity of the multitude: "Who are they and where have they come from?" A threefold answer is given: they have come out of the great tribulation, have washed their robes white in the blood of the Lamb, and therefore will enjoy the fullness of God's saving presence. In verse 9 of the opening chapter John has claimed to share with them the tribulation. Frequently the New Testament writers insist that the Christian life necessarily involves tribulation (Jn 16:33; Rom 5:3; 1 Pt 4:12) or a share in the sufferings of Jesus (Col 1:24), but both Old Testament and New Testament writers also speak of a period of intense tribulation before the parousia, a notion that seems to be in the author's mind here (Dn 12:1; Mt 24:21). The second characteristic of the multitude involves a mixing of metaphors — robes washed white in the Lamb's blood. This does not necessarily mean that all are martyrs. Rather, due to the redemptive sacrifice of Jesus, they are purified completely so that they can be in God's presence (1:5). In 3:4 dirty clothes symbolized unbelief, defection from Christ, and the worship of false gods. Now the priesthood of God's elect is fully realised, for they serve in his presence day and night (1:6).

God's final salvific activity is beautifully described in seven statements as the writer changes his tense from the present to the future. That God himself "will spread his tent over them," recalls the Exodus theme. This theme is found all through the

Apocalypse such as in the images of sealing and washing of robes. The verb used for "tenting" recalls the "shekinah" or protective presence of Yahweh dwelling with his people in the temple (Ex 40:34–38) and in Jesus (Jn 1:14). Now the dream of Ezek 37:27 becomes a reality: "My dwelling shall be with them; I will be their God and they shall be my people."

The next three statements promise that starvation, thirst, and the burning heat will be no more. Isaiah had prophesied a similar hope of liberation to the Babylonian exiles (Is 49:10). Further the Lamb, in a surprising reversal of roles, will shepherd them. This is the function of Yahweh himself in Ezek 34 and of the king in Ps 23. In the Fourth Gospel the Lamb of God is also the good shepherd (Jn 1:29; 10:14). Shepherding is a symbol of protection and guidance and security. He will guide them (the same verb is used of the Holy Spirit in Jn 16:13) to springs of living water. John's gospel has similar reflections:

> He who comes to me shall not hunger, and he who believes in me shall never thirst (6:35).
> If anyone thirsts let him come to me and let him who believes in me drink. As the scripture has said "out of his heart shall flow rivers of living water" (7:37f).

Finally, like a tender mother comforting with her handkerchief a tearful child, God himself will wipe away every tear from their eyes (Is 25:8; 1 Cor 15:54). Elizabeth Schüssler Fiorenza aptly comments —

> According to Revelation, final salvation does not just pertain to the soul and spiritual realities. It is the abolishment of all

dehumanization and suffering and at the same time the fullness of human well-being. The vision and promise of such ultimate well-being are thus clearly intended as a rectification of the great tribulation with its sufferings of war, peacelessness, hunger and inflation, pestilence, persecution, and death. The outcry of those who ask for justice and revenge of their lives is granted in this vision of eschatological well-being and salvation.

3). THE SEVENTH SEAL AND THE SOUNDING OF THE SEVEN TRUMPETS, 8:1–11:14

The opening of the seventh seal is typically surprising. We might have expected a terrifying end. Instead, the result is an anticlimax. In contrast to the joyful and ceaseless hymn which ended chapter 7 there is silence in heaven for about half an hour. This in turn leads to a new series of visions heralded by seven angels with trumpets, each followed by a vision of destruction brought upon a sinful world. In a similar interlocking literary device, when we come to the seventh trumpet, seven bowls will follow and the story is told again. Thus John in typical semitic fashion goes over the same ground in a cyclic pattern which contrasts sharply with our linear, logical, and climactic approach. Each time however he stresses different aspects like a great symphony repeating the same theme. He is not interested in just giving a message but in involving our imagination in a vast concentric spiral. He has moved from Patmos (ch 1) to Asia Minor (2–3) to the heavenly court (4-5) to the universe (6-10). The seven letters describe judgement and salvation from the point of view of seven particular communities. The seven seals emphasise the same theme from the point of view of all humanity while the seven trumpets take a more cosmic view. Each new series brings out new facets for our contemplation. Thus one must avoid the kind of chronological question which asks how a third of the light of the sun, moon, and stars can be darkened (8:12) when already in 6:13 they have been extinguished and the sky has disappeared.

The Seventh Seal, 8:1–5

The resulting silence has been variously interpreted as ominous, solemn, impressive or as a dramatic suspense builder, leading to a delayed judgement. Perhaps at the back of the author's thinking lie such Old Testament texts as Hb 2:20 where the whole earth is invited to keep silence before the Lord in his holy temple and to pray like Habakkuk that God in his coming wrath will remember his compassion (Zech 2:13; Zeph 1:7f). Another suggestion is Elijah's vision of God which has been an important model for the mystical life. The First Book of Kings (19:12) is best translated "there was a sound of silence" suggesting that God is not so much to be seen in the divinised forces of nature but that his mysterious presence is best sensed in silence and emptiness. The context suggests that the silence is emphasised to show that God is concerned to hear the prayers of those suffering in the great tribulation. However, the text does not stress the "hearing" of the prayers.

In addition to the silence John notes the presence of the seven angels who stand before God and the coming of the angel of incense. We know the names of the seven from biblical and extrabiblical sources: Michael from Daniel, Apocalypse and Jude; Gabriel from Daniel and Luke, Raphael from Tobit. The other four, Uriel, Raguel, Sariel, and Remiel are found in Enoch who names the seven archangels (1 Enoch 20:1–8; Is 63:9). Each name ends in "el," a Hebrew word for God, showing how each manifests some aspect of God's activity.

The whole scene is a reflection on the golden altar of incense which was in an open air court of the temple of Jerusalem. Luke (1:9) describes how Zechariah once carried out this task which involved the carrying of a fire pan filled with hot coals. These were heaped on the altar and incense was scattered on them, filling the whole court with clouds of fragrant smoke.

The angel with the censer hurling the coals of Yahweh's wrath onto the earth alludes to Ezek 10:2. There the person dressed in linen is instructed to go within the wheelwork under the cherubim, to fill his hands with burning coals and to scatter them over the city. John's suggestion is that the prayers of the faithful are important because they set ablaze the fire of God and cast it upon the earth. The result is thunder, rumblings, flashes of lightning, and an earthquake. The first four trumpet visions develop the idea of the fire cast on earth by the priest angel. This language recalls the appearance of Yahweh at Sinai and suggests that he has come once again to save his faithful (Ex 19:16–19). There too God had intervened to the accompaniment of a very loud thunder blast. The trumpet is the favourite instrument of the apocalyptic writers. There were, it seems, seven trumpets in the temple orchestra (Neh 12:41; 1 Chr 15:24), which were sounded on important occasions. The power of the trumpet was seen in the fall of Jericho (Jos 6:1–22). It was expected to announce the coming of the Day of Yahweh (Jl 2:1), the Lord's coming (1 Thes

4:16), the raising of the dead, and the beginning of the new era
(1 Cor 15:52; Mt 24:31).

There is an obvious parallel between the trumpet and the
seal vision. Both have four brief visions followed by two longer
ones and a seventh which is transitional. The suffering in the
trumpet visions is more extensive because one third of the
earth is affected in contrast to one fourth in 6:8. Neither,
obviously, are the final judgements of God. The purpose of the
trumpets which do not deal with the church as such but with
the world, is to give warning. The author is using material
drawn from the plagues which affected only Egypt, from
different Old Testament prophets, and from natural phenomena such as the nearby volcanic island of Thera which he
may have seen erupting. His approach is schematic. Each
trumpet leads to the destruction of three areas or aspects. His
aim is not to predict the future in detail but to paint a fiery
vivid picture as a warning of repentance for the present. This
picture is drawn from the past. In 15:3 the parousia is
compared to the Exodus which was anticipated by a series of
plagues, which likewise did not lead to repentance. The
biblical account of the plagues written long afterwards by
people who had never been in Egypt is really part of a long
reflection on the problem of the hardening of peoples' hearts
to God despite the evidence of the world — why we lose the
promised land! Plagues or sufferings should teach people. The
fantastic biblical description is not to describe historically how
God punished the Egyptians. Rather by displaying God's
power and the stupidity of people, he invites his community
to grow out of their slavery and accept God as the great
liberator. The effect of sin on the natural world is a common
biblical belief which has been developed in modern ecological

thinking. Likewise the destruction of even part of the natural world is closely associated with the punishment of the human race.

The First Four Trumpets, 8:6–13

The first trumpet causes hail and fire mingled with blood. This unusual combination recalls the violent thunderstorm with hail and lightning of the seventh plague in Egypt (Ex 9:24; Ps 18:13; Jl 2:30; Ac 2 :19). R.H.Charles and Swete point out that even as recently as 1901 Italy suffered from intense red rains caused by the red sands of the Sahara. Such unusual phenomena were naturally used by the biblical writers to typify the coming judgement of Yahweh. The "third" of the earth burnt up is not to be taken as a pure mathematical calculation. The point is that the destruction is limited. In the second, the horizon widens to include the salt water; in the third, the sweet water, and in the fourth, the sky.

With the second trumpet "something like a great mountain burning with fire was hurled into the sea" (v 8). This suggests a volcano such as the eruption of Vesuvius in A.D. 79 which destroyed Herculaneum and Pompeii in the bay of Naples. There is an allusion to the first Egyptian plague when the Nile was turned into blood and the fish destroyed. However, John's vision is of a much greater spectacle which involves the sea and ships.

With the third trumpet attention is directed from the sea to the waters on the land. A great star named "Wormwood," burning like a torch, falls from heaven and turns the fresh water bitter. In Jeremiah 23:15 God threatens to give the prophets wormwood (a very bitter herb) to eat and poison to drink because the prophets have filled the people with visions of their own fancy, with emptiness and ungodliness. For Amos wormwood is perverted justice. The falling star (of Babylon) may allude to Isaiah's taunt of Babylon's king (Is 14:12). For John, Babylon is Rome which has poisoned the springs of the land with her idolatry. Here we find the first reference to the loss of human life in the plagues. But there is still time for the others to repent.

The fourth plague (8:12) strikes the heavenly bodies. The partial darkness recalls the darkness in Egypt in the ninth plague (Ex 10:21–23). Darkness was closely associated with judgement and disaster (Am 8:9; Mk 13:24; Mt 27:45). Typically John now introduces a new element to surprise his reader, an eagle crying out a triple woe: the last three plagues. In contrast to the first four, these three are aimed directly at the inhabitants of the earth. The solitary eagle with its piercing screech, circling in the sky in the sight of all, waiting to swoop on its prey, is a familiar occurrence in the East. The eagle is a bird of prey and is often a symbol of disaster (Mt 24:28). The interpretation here seems to involve a surprising reversal of the Exodus motif. In Ex 19:4 Yahweh tells the Israelites: "You have seen for yourselves how I treated the Egyptians and how I bore you on eagle wings and brought you here to myself." Instead the message is one of "Woe" and chastisement. Frequently in the Old Testament the eagle or vulture symbolises an invading army used as an instrument of Yahweh who works through the political powers of the world to discipline his people (Hab 1:8; Deut 28:19). But the phrase "inhabitants of the earth" is normally distinguished from the faithful (3:10). One of the four living creatures in 4:7 had a face like a flying eagle.

The Fifth Trumpet, 9:1–11

T.F. Glasson, commenting in *The Cambridge Bible Commentary* on chapter 9, remarks that few commentators have been able to discover much spiritual or literary value in this chapter. He has the impression that the writer is content to pile horror upon horror in order somehow to fill out his numerical scheme of seven. However, not all would agree with this estimate of the deliberately repulsive and bizarre imagery which John recounts in this chapter. With the last three trumpets he moves into the realm of the spirit and of evil just as he does when treating the last three seals. John is not writing a document for non-Christians to read. His aim is to lead his community to repentance, to invite people to draw closer to God as they witness the chastening disasters of the world. What he is struggling to say is a message not unlike that of modern psychologists like Carl Jung. These scholars insist that contemporary people are often blind to the fact that, despite their rationality and efficiency, they are possessed by demonic forces that are beyond their control. The ancient demons and gods have not disappeared at all but have merely received new names. They keep people on the run with restlessness, alienation, vague apprehensions, psychological complications, an insatiable need for pills, alcohol, tobacco, food and, above all, a wide array of personal and political and international neuroses. The commentator Thomas F. Torrance compares the preaching of the word of God to the star which falls from Heaven and opens the bottomless pit of human nature. The result of preaching the Gospel is that "either men are ashamed and converted or the bottomless pit is opened." Surely that is what has happened to the western world, in the land of Dachau or of the Gulags, for example.

The Cross of Jesus Christ has provoked such a reaction against it that all the latent evil in people has been pushed to the surface in unbelievable wickedness and bloodshed. The very bottomless pit has been opened in our midst, so that heaven and earth have been darkened with its fumes and the whole atmosphere of the world has been poisoned.

John is careful to insist that only at the angel's trumpet blast and only when God gives the key is the abyss of evil opened. The God of the Lamb is firmly in control, and the suffering of the first woe only lasts five months, the lifetime of a locust plague. The parallel with the permission given to Satan to test the faith of Job seems evident. The idea of the fallen angel was a very popular "original sin" story among the Jewish people (Gn 6:1ff; Is 14:12). Jesus' statement that he saw Satan fall like a star from heaven shows the common view that the stars were angels (1:20). Here we find, for the first time in the book, the idea of the pit of the abyss which is at the antithesis of the heavenly court. In the book of Enoch this is the place where the spirits, which had rebelled against God, are imprisoned. In 11:7 and 17:8 John describes the abyss as the place from which the wild beast comes up to wage war. In Romans 10:7 it is the realm of the dead and in Luke 8:31 a prison for demons.

The scene is like a horror film. From the abyss comes billowing smoke which clouds the sun and fills the air as the infernal army pours out. Locusts, the most commonly mentioned insects in the Old Testament, are symbolically used there for hostile hosts (e.g. the Midianites Jdg 6:5). A plague of locusts is one of the most disastrous scourges to strike a country. Countless grasshoppers are involved, flying with a most frightful noise as they completely strip the vegetation of the countryside. According to Dt 28:33 such a plague was a

punishment from Yahweh. The eighth plague which struck
the Eyptians is in mind here (Ex 10:13-15). But it is the Book
of Joel which inspires the vision of the invading locusts here
— their teeth, the flight, their warlike garland, the comparison
with war horses (Jl 1:6; 2:4f). Clearly no normal locusts are
involved because unlike normal locusts they do not eat grass.
They are like horses equipped for battle. Their chests are like
breastplates. They have golden crowns on their heads like
kings, human faces and hair like women, teeth like lion's teeth,
and tails with stings like scorpions. Various allusions can be
detected in this horrible and bizarre scene. The dreaded
enemy from the East, the Parthians, wore long hair. But John's
purpose is to describe the rampant but organised onslaught of
the powers of evil on the world. Their king was the angel of
the abyss called Abaddon in Hebrew and Apollyon in Greek
— both mean destroyer. The Hebrew term is the equivalent
of Sheol in Job 28:22, or it simply means destruction (Job
26:6). The use of the Greek word Apollyon is perhaps an
indirect attack on Domitian who claimed to be the incarnate
Apollo; the locust was one of the symbols of the Greek god
Apollo. But the fact that the locusts cannot attack those who
have God's seal on their forehead (v 4) shows that the torment
is purely spiritual and that the writer has in mind a purely
symbolic interpretation.

The Sixth Trumpet, 9:13–21

The picture of destruction is greatly intensified with the sixth
trumpet. In contrast to the five month's torture by the locusts,
a third of the world's population is wiped out. Instead of an
army of strange locust-like creatures, there are 200 million

fire-breathing horses and riders; the total for both sides in World War II was about 70 million.

The command comes from between the horns of the golden altar which stood in God's presence. The horns suggest God's power and control. The altar recalls the prayers of the faithful at the altar of incense (8:3f) and suggests that God's judgement on their sufferings is being carried out. This trumpet releases the four angels who were held bound at the river Euphrates. They in turn lead into battle a devastating horde of riders clad in fiery red, deep blue, and pale yellow. But their horses or perhaps dragons are even more deadly with heads like lions, mouths spewing fire, sulphur and smoke, and tails like deadly snakes, sent to slay a third of all people. The Euphrates or the great river, as the Old Testament often calls it, was not only the ideal boundary of the promised land (Gn 15:18) but also the boundary between the Roman Empire and the feared Parthians. Israel's enemies often came from this area (16:12; Jer 2:18).

The final two verses of chapter 9 insist that God's purpose in the suffering and terror of the plagues was to lead people to repentance (2:5; 21:24) because of the idols which they had made with their hands. No matter what God does, people tend to cling to their demon worship. In 1 Cor 10:20 Paul also joins demons with idols (see also 2 Cor 6:14ff).

The biblical writers are not very "ecumenical" in the scorn they tend to cast on the foolishness of other religions and their cultic objects of gold, silver, bronze, stone, and wood which can neither see, hear nor walk (Is 17:8; Dt 5:23; Ps 115:4–7; 135:15-17). It takes but little imagination to apply this criticism to the materialism, decadence, and in particular, the nuclear weapons of modern society. Paul too insists that, unless one worships the right god, any type of evil or sin is possible (Rom 1:24ff). Twice more John lists sins in 21:8; 22:15. But the particular four here are unique among the New Testament lists (Mk 7:21f; Gal 5:19ff). Three of the four are sins against the commandments of not murdering, committing adultery or stealing. The second, in Greek, "pharmakeia," literally means the use of drugs, sorcery, or magic arts or witchcraft (Ex 7:11) which were strongly condemned in the Old Testament (Dt 18:11).

The Mighty Angel and the Little Scroll, 10:1–11

After hearing the six trumpet blasts we are now keyed up to hear the seventh. But a new intermediary further heightens the tension. As he did before the seventh seal, the author inserts an interlude or an introduction to keep readers in suspense, to encourage the faithful after such a presentation of disasters, and to prepare them for the final climactic disaster. This brief chapter mentions the seventh trumpet in v 7, but the actual blowing of the seventh trumpet does not come until 11:15.

John begins with a vivid and dramatic description of a mighty angel coming down from heaven. The scene is back on earth again at Patmos. The majestic vision of the cloud, the rainbow around his head, his face shining like the sun and legs like pillars of fire recalls the majestic vision of Christ in the opening chapter. The cosmic harmony of cloud, rainbow, sun, and fire suggesting the covenant with Noah contrasts sharply with the destructive forces in the previous chapters. This angel, which resembles the famous Colossus of Rhodes, one of the seven wonders of the ancient world, descends like God himself in the Exodus tradition (Ex 13:32). In 9:1 the star was said to fall from heaven. The angel, who is God's special representative, shares in the glory of God himself. In Sirach 50:7 the high priest Simon can be compared to the sun and the rainbow. The voice of the angel is like that of God himself —it is like the roaring of the lion and associated with the voices of the seven thunders (Am 3:4; Jn 12:27ff). But, in one of John's typically unexpected paradoxes, this mighty angel holds a little open scroll which contrasts with the sealed scroll in chapter 5. He takes an oath that the delay of the end will be no more.

John is about to write the message of the seven thunders (God himself!) but he is suddenly prohibited by a voice from heaven: "Seal up what the seven thunders have spoken and do not write it down." This unusual prohibition has led to a variety of interpretations. The cryptic phrase "seal up" recalls the command to Daniel to "seal the book until the end of time; many shall fall away and evil shall increase" (Dn 12:4). Daniel's message was not for his contemporaries and it was written down. John's message was for his contemporaries and although he is usually concerned to share it, this part is not written down. One suggestion is that John is referring to the date of the parousia and that he is emphasising that no one can know it (Mk 13:32). Therefore, only a partial revelation is given to John's audience. Another suggestion is that a personal message of comfort is involved, such as that which Paul received when he was raised to the third heaven in 2 Cor 12:4. Does it mean that further woes are announced but cancelled by God? Some scholars take the sealed scroll to represent the Old Testament and the little scroll presented by one like Christ to be the Gospel, the fulfillment of the Old Testament (10:7). Perhaps it is best to take chapter 10 as an introduction to what follows and to accept that we do not fully understand John's meaning here.

Suspecting that his readers are disturbed by a seemingly indefinite delay, John's angel raises his right hand (a synonym for swearing: Dn 12:7; Gn 14:22), and swears by God, the eternal creator, that "there shall be no more delay" (Dn 12:6). When the seventh trumpet sounds, "the mysterious plan of God, which he announced to his servants the prophets will be fulfilled." John is writing towards the end of the first century when the early hopes of an imminent parousia seem to have disappeared and a solemn assurance was needed (2 Pt 3:3ff). Some older translations gave the impression that John was making a rather profound philosophical statement that eternity will have begun: "Time will be no more." But the proper translation is "There shall be no more delay." With the seventh trumpet the final purposes of God will be completed, that is, the judgements of the bowls and the final establishment of God's kingdom. The mystery (1:20) is the good news that the kingdom belongs to Christ forever (11:15) and that Satan will be overthrown (20:10).

The voice speaks again and bids John to take and "devour" the little scroll which will be "sour in your stomach but in your mouth will taste sweet as honey." This scene, inspired by the vocation of Ezekiel (3:3; Jer 15:16), confirms John's vocation and reminds him that he "must prophesy again for many peoples and nations, languages and kings." The kings are dealt with in chapters 13 and 17. The bitter-sweet paradox (Prov 20:17; Job 20:12–14) seems to say that although God's words are a joy and a delight (Jer 15:16), the experience of absorbing them is bitter medicine not only for the prophet but also for his audience. Ezekiel's sweet message consisted of "lamentation and mourning and woe" especially against Jerusalem, but there was no reference to its bitterness for the prophet. However John's message in the following chapter will likewise describe the devastation of Jerusalem. John's message, like Jeremiah's (Jer 1:10), is not limited to the Church or to any one group but has consequences for all countries and empires, for kings and for people.

The Preservation of the Faithful — The Two Witnesses, 11:1–14

Everybody has their favourite difficult chapter in the Apocalypse. But this chapter must rate near the top of all lists. However, it is an important one because it introduces the key themes of the remaining chapters: the beast, the killing of the faithful witnesses, the great city, the resurrection, the judgement of the dead, and the final reward. Thus in John's unusual style of writing, which is thematic rather than chronological, he again gives a summary of his whole story, a kind of prophetic overview of the remainder of his book.

Hitherto the writer has been a rather passive spectator of the divine dimension and activity. Now that the angel has bridged the gap by placing his feet on the sea and the land and by commissioning the prophet (10:2,9), John becomes more actively involved. Eating the bitter scroll brings a judgement which leads to the measuring of the temple, the counting of the worshippers, the raising of the two witnesses, and the triumph of God's kingdom.

Recent scholars tend to give a symbolic interpretation to the early verses of this chapter. An opposing view is the attempt of John A.T. Robinson (*Redating the New Testament*, pp 238ff) to revive the nineteenth century view that the book as a whole was written before the destruction of the temple in A.D. 70. The passage insists that only a tenth of the city falls after the assumption of the two witnesses and this, not by the attack of the enemy, but by an earthquake (v 13). He sees the command to measure as meaning the purification of the actual temple. This is associated with the final call for repentance by the two witnesses.

The idea of measuring the temple is found in both the Old Testament and in nonbiblical literature with a variety of meanings including restoration and rebuilding, destruction and judgement, and preservation from physical and spiritual harm (Ezek 40:3ff; 1 En 61:1–5). The purpose here is to protect the (Christian) worshippers. The outer courtyard is not measured but is given over to the (non-Christian) people who will trample the holy city (the Church) for forty-two months. The word "trample" probably means persecute, just as Antiochus had persecuted the Jewish people during Maccabean times (Dn 8:10).

Three equivalent periods of time are mentioned: 42 months, the reign of the beast(13:5); 1,260 days (or 42 months of 30 days) (11:3); and three and one half days or a time, times (dual form) and a half time where a day or a time equals a year (12:14; 13:5). The background is found in Hosea 6:2, which describes the rebirth of the people, and especially in Daniel 7:25; 12:7, which describes the sufferings under Antiochus from June 168/7 B.C. to December 165/4 B.C. Thus the numbers 42, 1260, and 3½ are all ways of describing a definite period of tribulation until God delivers his people. But according to John, because the faithful worship in the temple, they seem to be exempt from the suffering of the tribulation. However, the measuring of the temple is just a brief introduction to the account of the two witnesses who do suffer.

The identity of the two witnesses, who are commissioned to prophesy in sackcloth, is quite vague because significantly our author does not name them. Hippolytus and Tertullian suggested Enoch and Elijah, who were expected at the end of time. Victorinus in his commentary suggested Jeremiah and Elijah. Others suggest Christian martyrs such as James of Jerusalem and John the Apostle or more especially Peter and Paul martyred by Nero the beast.

The content deals with the same basic story which is found repeated over and over again in the Apocalypse. Persecution of the Christians leads to final judgement on the persecutors and to salvation for the faithful. The two witnesses are symbolically described, "the two olive trees and the two lampstands," identification which calls to mind the two Messiahs of Zechariah's vision, the new high priest Joshua (Zech 6:11–13) and the new Davidic prince Zerubbabel (Zech 4:1ff). These lived about 520 B.C. during the time of restoration after the Babylonian captivity. The meaning seems to be that a new period of restoration is to be expected as the faithful give witness to the gospel. John appears to use a familiar story from the past to interpret his current situation and to describe the power and protection available to God's witnesses. Their witnessing ministry is described in terms that recall not only the marvellous deeds of Moses and Elijah but also the life, death, ascension, and vindication of Jesus himself. Their power to devour their foes by fire and to close up the sky so that no rain will fall during their mission, recalls the biblical accounts of Elijah (2 Kgs 1:9–12; 1 Kgs 17–18; Sir 48:3; Lk 4:25; Jam 5:17). Their power to turn water into blood and to afflict the earth with plagues would remind the reader of

Moses' plagues and especially the turning of the Nile and other waters into blood (Ex 7:14–19). The killing of the witnesses in Jerusalem where "their Lord was crucified," the corpses stared at unburied for three and a half days, God's returning the breath of life to them, their ascension in a cloud, the earthquake — all parallel the ministry of Jesus, his mighty deeds, his death, resurrection and ascension. Elijah also ascended as did Moses according to tradition (2 Kgs 2:11; Jude v 9). The teaching of the passage seems to be that the Church will be protected by God for a sufficient time to fulfil its mission of witness. Many will be killed and the gloating opposition will seem to triumph. But God will enable his people to achieve ultimate triumph.

Almost casually, as if the author is reacting to a story well known to his audience, he introduces the wild beast, who is coming up from the abyss to kill the witnesses, (v 7). The beast, the personification of evil, who is also called Satan, the dragon, and the devil, is mentioned about forty times in the rest of the book and will be treated more fully in chapters 13 and 17. The background is Daniel's fourth beast from the sea, which represents the evil empire and the ideology which the faithful must endure.

The place of their ministry and death is the holy city (11:2) also called "the great city whose name 'pneumatikos' is Sodom or Egypt." The Greek word "pneumatikos" is sometimes translated "allegorically" but probably a translation such as "symbolically," "prophetically," or "spiritually," is better. A number of Old Testament passages clarify the symbolism. Isaiah (1:10) criticizes the rulers and people of Judah and Jerusalem by likening them to the inhabitants of Sodom, a symbol of the stubborn rejection of God (Mk 10:15). Ezekiel

condemns the Jewish people for remembering Egypt, the place
of oppression, and the lewdness and harlotry found there (Ez
23:27). Already John had called the Jews at Smyrna and
Philadelphia a synagogue of Satan (3:9). For John, Babylon,
Sodom, Egypt, Jerusalem and Rome are all of a kind. Wherever there is rejection of God and his Lamb, there they are to
be found. In simple fact the choice is between two versions of
the same city. Jerusalem the holy and Jerusalem the sinner.
Jerusalem is every city, person, or country.

T.F.Torrance makes a devastating comment on the comfort
of many modern Christians, a comment which catches very
well the author's point:

> Why does the Church of Jesus Christ today sit so easy to her
> surroundings? Why do Christian people live such comfortable
> and such undisturbed lives in this evil and disturbed world?
> Surely it is because we are not true to the Word of God.

Faithful witness, according to John, leads to rampant and
seemingly triumphant evil. The people of the earth gloat over
the corpses of the witnesses and in an ultimate humiliation
refuse them the dignity of burial (Tob 1:18ff; Ps 79:3-4). In
their merriment they exchange gifts because the prophets'
messages were a torment to the whole earth. But God's answer
is resurrection. The passage recalls Ezekiel's vision of the
raising of the dry bones of Israel (Ezek 37:5-12).

The earthquake, a symbol of God's powerful presence and
judgement, leads not to the total destruction of the city, but to
only a tenth of it, and the death of seven thousand people. The
rest through fear are led to worship the God of heaven — in
16:9 there is the opposite response. For John, to fear God and

give him glory is at the centre of the Gospel announced to all the peoples of the earth (14:6f; 15:4). These texts show that John is not advocating a mere theology of vindictive justice. Rather he advocates a theology of hope, of hope in the final conversion of the world based on the final saving intervention of God.

Now having given us an interlude from 10:1–11:13, John reminds us that the second woe has passed, and he returns us to the trumpet cycle. The seventh trumpet is the proclamation of the kingdom. But it is also the third woe which is "coming soon" to bring God's wrath to the raging nations and his destruction to those who destroy the earth.

With the opening of the seventh seal, instead of describing the final judgement as we might have expected, John surprises us with a period of silence, and from this silence comes the trumpet cycle. Now with the seventh trumpet we are still left in suspense. Instead of silence we are given a chorus of loud voices rejoicing in God's kingship (11:15) leading into a series of unnumbered visions in which scholars have found different patterns of seven. Cardinal J.H. Newman in his *Parochial and Plain Sermons* (vi, 240f) makes the illuminating comment that although time intervenes between Christ's first and second coming, it is not recognized in the Gospel scheme

> but is, as it were, an accident. For so it was that up to Christ's coming in the flesh, the course of things ran straight towards that end, nearing it by every step; but now, under the Gospel, that course has (if I may so speak) altered its direction, as regards His second coming, and runs, not towards the end, but along it and on the brink of it; and is at all times equally near that great event, which did it run towards, it would at once run

into Christ, then, is ever at our doors; as near eighteen hundred years ago as now, and not nearer now than then; and not nearer when he comes than now. When he says he will come 'soon' it is not a word of time but of natural order. This present state of things, "the present distress" as St. Paul calls it, is ever close upon the next world and resolves itself into it. As when a man is given over, he may die at any moment yet lingers; as an implement of war may any moment explode, and must at some time; as we listen for a clock to strike, and at length it surprises us; as a crumbling arch hangs, we know not how, and is not safe to pass under; so creeps on this feeble, weary world, and, one day, before we know where we are, it will end.

Typically John skips over the description of the last woe to introduce a heavenly vision and liturgical scene. He might agree with Coleridge's saying that anticipation is more important than surprise. This liturgy provides a summary and anticipation of the remaining chapter of the book while it develops some of the themes announced earlier. The rage of the nations has led to God's superior rage (12:12; 14:7; 20:11–15). Now the "kairos," or time (1:3), has come. This time or "kairos" means judgement of the dead (20:11–15), the reward of the prophetic servants, the saints who revere God both great and small (21:1–4; 22:3–5), and destruction of the destroyers (19:2ff; 20:10).

In the hymn found in chapter 5 the Lamb was acclaimed as worthy to rule. Now the hymn of the twenty-four elders celebrates the fact that the reign is begun. The reign is the key theme of the book (1:6). Such verses as 11:15; 19:6 and 16 inspired the tremendous joyful chorus of Handel, the Hallelujah Chorus.

The phrases "Why do the nations rage?" and the "Lord and his anointed" allude to Psalm 2 which describes the claim of the Israelite kings to world dominion and emphasises the futility of rebellious plotting against God's plans. This heavenly scene provides a significant background and introduction to the dreadful beast scenes to come, just as chapters 4 and 5 introduced the two vision cycles.

Almighty God is significantly described from now on (16:5) as the one "who is and who was" without the future dimension to insist that the kingdom is already present despite the beast-like empire which seems ascendant.

The heavenly singing leads to the temple in heaven being again laid open. A story is told that the composer Elgar was very happy with a friend's reply to his question as to what he thought of his musical arrangement of "Praise to the Holiest in the Height" in *The Dream of Gerontius*: "It makes me think of heavenly doors opening and shutting." Now it is not the altar but the ark of the covenant that becomes visible. Again the sense is symbolic. In 21:22 we will be told that in the heavenly city there is no need for a temple to symbolize God's presence. The ark or chest which God ordered Moses to construct (Ex 25:10–22) was probably destroyed when Nebuchadnezzar burned the temple in 586 B.C. According to Jeremiah it would no longer be missed in the Messianic days (Jer 3:16; 2 Macc 2:4). For it was a symbol of Yahweh's protection and was even used as a war palladium (1 S 4:1–9). The vision here is well placed just before John describes the terrible onslaught of evil in the stories of the woman, the dragon, and the two beasts. Not surprisingly, the ark is accompanied by lightning, noises, thunder, earthquake, and hail, the typical earthly accompaniments of Yahweh's intervention and pronouncements.

4) THE VISION OF THE WOMAN, THE DRAGON, AND THE TWO BEASTS, 12:1–14:20

Here John gives us an imaginary description of the eschatological heavenly conflict which he introduced in 11:7 when he — described the emergence of the wild beast from the abyss to conquer and kill the faithful. A new theme or emphasis on signs is now described for the first time in the book. Some seven signs in all are described from chapters 12 — 19, three heavenly (12:1,3; 15:1) and four on earth (13:13f; 16:14; 19:20). Only the first is a good sign, whereas the rest are signs of judgement and evil. John is trying to deal with the age-old question why the faithful are being persecuted (3:10). Satan — and his agents, Rome and its emperor cult, are the culprits. But — his message is one of hope. The Lamb standing on Mt. Sion — had already triumphed over the beasts. These three chapters between the end of the trumpet visions and the beginning of the bowl visions form a certain unity. But there is little agreement on the detailed plan of the author.

For convenience we can divide these three chapters into seven signs or visions.

(i)	The Woman Clothed with the Sun	12:1–2
(ii)	The Huge Red Dragon	12:3–17
(iii)	The Beast from the Sea	13:1–10
(iv)	The Second Beast from the Land	13:11–18
(v)	The Lamb and his Companions on Sion	14:1–5
(vi)	The Three Angels Announcing Judgement	14:6-13
(vii)	The Harvest of the Earth	14:14–20

i) The Woman Clothed with the Sun, 12:1–2

A great sign appears in the sky. Sin by contrast comes from the lowest region, the abyss. The term "sign" in the Old Testament signifies an event which reveals a divine intervention for confirmation or reassurance or protection (Is 7:10ff; Ex 7:3). Like the two witnesses in chapter 11 the woman seems to be a corporate or collective figure rather than an individual one. The woman is the community of believers from whom the Messiah came. This community is first of all the Old Testament people of God. But, secondly, it includes the New Testament faithful who have given birth to Jesus' brothers and sisters. In the Old Testament the image of a woman in travail is a key symbol for Israel (Is 66:7; Mic 4:10). The birth pangs symbolize the troubled times through which the messianic age is being born. Isaiah, for example, thus describes the failure of Israel to achieve salvation:

> O Lord oppressed by your punishment,
> we cried out in anguish under your chastising.
> As a woman about to give birth
> writhes and cries out in her pains,
> so were we in your presence, O Lord.
> We conceived and writhed in pain,
> giving birth to wind.
> Salvation we have not achieved for the earth,
> the inhabitants of the world cannot bring it forth.
> But your dead shall live, their corpses shall rise. (Is 26:16–19)

The woman is described as a sun goddess, with the moon under her feet and the twelve constellations of the zodiac as her crown, signifying her power over the destinies of the people. This description recalls Canticle 6:10 but more precisely the dream of Joseph in Genesis 37:9. There the sun symbolizes Jacob and Israel, the moon Rachael, and the twelve stars the twelve sons of Jacob who founded the tribes of Israel. According to Hippolytus (c 230) "The woman clothed with the sun" clearly symbolises the Church clothed with the Father's Word who shines more brilliantly than the sun. "The moon beneath her feet" shows that she, like the moon, is adorned with heavenly glory. "A crown of stars on her head" signifies the apostles through whom the Church was founded. Her travail shows that the Church never ceases begetting from her heart the Word who is being persecuted by the unbelievers of the world. The conflict between the woman and the serpent recalls the description of the struggle between the serpent and the woman's seed in Gn 3:15. Not surprisingly, the Fathers of the Church and Church art and liturgy from the fourth century onwards identified the woman not only with the persecuted Church but also with Mary the mother of the Messiah.

ii) The Huge Red Dragon, 12:3–17

A second wonder or sign is now seen in the sky, the great red dragon. Dragon translates the Hebrew word "tannin" used in Genesis 1:21 for the great sea monsters, in Exodus 7:9 for the serpent into which Aaron's rod was turned, and in Deuteronomy 32:33 where the wine of God's foes is compared to the venom of dragons. Psalm 74:13–15 speaks of God's smashing the heads of the dragons and of the monster Leviathan. John's dragon with its many heads, horns, and diadems recalls Daniel's beast with ten horns (Dn 7:7). Daniel's beast resembles in many ways the mythological beast Leviathan which

symbolises the Greek empire under Alexander and his successors, particularly the Seleucid king Antiochus IV who persecuted the Jewish religion. Thus John prepares the way for the
dragon's minions, the two beasts who symbolise the Roman
empire and religion in chapter 13. Significantly, some of the
Roman cohorts used the sign of the dragon as a military
emblem. Jeremiah compared the Babylonian Nebuchadnezzar
to a dragon as also Pharaoh was described by Ezekiel (Jer
51:34; Ezek 29:3).

The struggle between the woman giving birth to the ruler
of "all the nations with an iron scepter" (2:27) and the dragon
who stood before her (Gn 3:14) recalls the ancient story in
Biblical and Near Eastern mythology of the struggle with the
sea monster (Is 27:1). The child arrives and is protected by
God and enthroned in heaven. Venerable Bede (d 735)
interpreted the child as a reference to the Church. But many
early interpreters such as Tyconius (d 390) saw the reference
both to Christ and to his members, the Church. Just as Daniel
seems to move between a collective and an individual interpretation of the Son of Man, so John fuses the reign of Christ and
the Church (1:5f). The power of the dragon is not so great that
he can sweep a considerable number of the stars of heaven
with him. This may be a reference to the traditional story of
the angel's fall. Or from an analogy with Dn 8:10,24 the
reference may be not to fallen angels but to God's saints or
people who are trampled by Satan. The flight of the woman
into the desert for a time (11:2) parallels the experience of the
Exodus where the Israelites fled from Pharaoh. This theme is
further developed in v 13ff. The desert is the place of safety, of
God's care, of his testing and discipline of the chosen people.

In common with the ancient mythology, John now portrays the conflict between good and evil in terms of a great heavenly primeval battle. In Enuma Elish, a Babylonian creation myth, Marduk the god of light slays Tiamat the seven-headed water dragon to produce the material creation. An Egyptian myth describes how the red dragon Set pursues the goddess Isis but is killed by her son Horus when he grows up. The Greek myth of the pregnant goddess Leto, escaping from the dragon Python to the island of Delos, is probably the closest to John's version. In the Greek story Leto gives birth to Apollo, who after four days finds Python in his cave and kills him. Another interesting parallel is with the Emperor Domitian about A.D. 83. Coinage shows how Domitian deified his dead ten-year-old son and his mother, calling her the mother of the gods and presenting his son as lord of the stars who will usher in the age of universal salvation. John is perhaps adapting such images to present Christ as the true ascended and risen Lord who is the saviour of the world. John uses contemporary imagery to proclaim a message of hope to his contemporaries in a difficult situation, to insist once again that Jesus is God's good news.

The red dragon, John insists, is none other than "the ancient serpent called the Devil or Satan, the seducer of the whole world" (v 9). Thus he equates the serpent from the garden of Eden with Satan even though Genesis does not make that connection. The strategy of the evil dragon is deception or seduction and he has a world-wide success. The opposing army of angels in the cosmic battle is led by the archangel Michael ("One who is like God"), Israel's patron saint, who was expected to stand up for the people in the final battle (Dn 12:1). The background to this scene is the Jewish story of the evil angels' fall from heaven (Gn 6:1-4; 1 Enoch

6-19; Jubilees 5; Adam and Eve 12-17). One might expect a description of a mighty battle but no weapons or fatalities are described. The victory is without weapons. Further, the first impression, that it is Michael not the Messiah who wins the battle is corrected by the key hymn (vv 10-12) which the author inserts.

This anonymous hymn, which is a shout of victory, insists first of all that the dragon did not succeed. The evil against which the Christians are struggling is already a beaten power in retreat after a decisive loss in battle. Salvation, power, and kingdom belong to God and authority to his Christ (9:3ff), not to anyone else. Three times the expression "cast out" or "cast down" is used of Satan the accuser of our brothers and sisters (Lk 10:18; Jn 12:31). He had accused Job (Jb 1:6) and Joshua the high priest (Zech 3:1) and now constantly accuses the faithful. As Paul wrote to the Romans:

> Who shall bring a charge against God's chosen ones? God
> who justifies? Who shall condemn them? Christ Jesus,
> who died or rather was risen up, who is at the right hand
> of God and who intercedes for us? (Rom 8:33f).

John even dares to say that our brothers and sisters defeated Satan. This was accomplished not by their own power but by "the blood of the Lamb and by (the help of) the word of their witness and because love for life did not deter them from death" (Mk 8:35f; Jn 12:25). Thus the victory hymn is an invitation to John's community to do the same and to imitate Christ's witness even unto death. Michael is only the heavenly symbol and the anticipation of the victory on earth.

The song is an invitation to the victors to rejoice. But the inhabitants of the earth and sea should be prepared for woe because the devil has come down.Although his fury has no limits, "his time is short" (1:3).

The purpose of the insertion of the brief hymn by John is to help his community to cope with the troubles to come. In his book *Man's Search for Meaning* (Hodder and Stoughton, 1963), Victor Frankl emphasises that similar goal-setting enabled some of the prisoners to survive the uncertainty and fears of life in the concentration camp. He stresses that a prisoner who had lost faith in the future was doomed because he or she fell into decline and became subject to mental and physical decay. To help a prisoner fight the influence of the concentration camps, one had to point to a future goal toward which one could look. This gave a prisoner inner strength.

After his brief hymn John returns to earth to his real purpose which is to help his readers cope with suffering on earth. The purpose of a myth is to explain the present reality through an imaginative story. The dragon of evil can harm only the woman and her child on earth, not those in heaven. But the child is now in heaven. The woman pursued into the desert recalls the Exodus motif and God's protective care when he bore the people on eagle's wings (Ex 19:4; Deut 32:11f). The desert was the place to escape to, the place of refuge from tyranny. The dragon causes a flood but God uses the earth to swallow it up and save the woman. The flood may symbolise the flood of evil which threatens to engulf the whole world. The earth is used by God to swallow up and punish evil (Num 26:10; Dt 11:6; Ps 106:16-18). The enraged dragon goes off to make war on the rest of her offspring "those who keep God's commandments and give witness to Jesus" (11:7; Mt 25:40; 16:18). The chapter ends with the angry, frustrated dragon standing on the sand of the sea about to call his lieutenants into action, beginning with the beast from the sea.

iii) The Beast from the Sea, 13:1–10

The previous chapter highlighted the struggle of the Christian community to give birth to the Messiah, the protection of God, and the diabolic opposition of the dragon, the ancient tempter. The suggestion is that a new creation is taking place as God once again conquers the chaotic forces of evil. In this chapter the struggle is not directly between God and the (defeated) dragon. The scene is now the earth in Asia Minor, and the struggle is between the faithful and the dragon's minions, the beasts. These are similar to the description of Leviathan and Behemoth of Job 40, 41 which were drawn from images of the crocodile and hippopotamus. But for John the source is Satan. He has already insisted that the Jewish synagogues at Smyrna and Philadelphia are "synagogues of Satan" whose throne is found at Pergamum (2:13).

The emergence of the beast (briefly mentioned in 11:7) from the Mediterranean Sea would suggest the regular coming of the conquering Roman proconsul from Rome which lay far beyond their horizon to the West. The sea had a profound symbolic meaning similar to their interpretation of the "abyss" in Genesis 1:2. While the earth symbolised God's creation and harmony, the sea suggested chaos, evil powers, and unredeemed humanity, as Swete commented:

> the seething cauldron of national and social life, out of which the great historical movements of the world arise.

John, gazing at the sea from Patmos, hopes for the day of Christ's victory when there will be no longer any sea or demonic opposition to God and his people (9:2; 21:1; Is 7:12).

To produce his picture of consummate evil, John combines

nearly all the features of Daniel's four beasts, which symbolise four successive beastly empires of evil. The ten horns were on Daniel's fourth beast, the third was leopard-like, the second like a bear, the first like a lion (Dn 7:24). The third beast had four heads, giving the four a total of seven. In John's time the fourth beast was often interpreted to symbolise the Roman Empire. Like the Roman Empire, John's beast has dominion over the whole earth, is worshipped by many people, and attacks the faithful (v 4, 7, 8). This identification would have been quite obvious to anyone in John's audience. He uses symbols to convey a sense of mysterious power and knowledge.

While the dragon is the great opponent of God (though not his equal), the sea beast is portrayed as a parody of the Lamb and all that Christ stands for; especially true Christian discipleship. Both have horns (power), but use swords, and both were slain. The same Greek word is used of both their deaths. Both rise to new life and authority over all peoples and kings. As Christ shares his Father's throne, so does the beast the power of Satan. John is attempting to describe the typical problem of church/state relations in every age, where the state so easily takes over the religious dimension to become a totalitarian state. This was particularly evident in the case of the Roman Emperor and the empire of his day.

John's warning to his community is the old message of the Exodus. The Pharaoh or emperor or state is not divine. The existence of Israel and the Church point to a higher allegiance and show up those powers who would stand in God's place and demand total allegiance. John is much more sensitive to the evil power and influence of the Roman Empire than Paul in Romans 13:1ff. 1 Peter 5:8-9 calls not for rebellion but for spiritual resistance by the willingness to share in Christ's suffering in a spirit of faith and hope (1 Pt 1:3-9; 2:13ff; 4:13). John does not call for loyalty towards Rome; neither does he issue a call for rebellion or vengeance. Rather, he insists on faithful endurance, on a willingness to suffer while fleeing into the wilderness when necessary (12:6, 14; 13:10; 14:12). Rome, the beast and prostitute with its satanic cult, will be destroyed and God will take vengeance (13; 17; 18:2).

The first beast is often referred to as the Antichrist, although the term is not found in the Apocalypse but is peculiar to the Johannine Epistles in the New Testament (1 Jn 2:18ff). According to Mark (13:21ff) Jesus himself had warned about the need for constant watchfulness because "false Christs and false prophets will appear performing signs and wonders to mislead, if it were possible, even the chosen." In 2 Thess 2:3, 9, Paul warned about the danger of seduction and the man of lawlessness, the son of perdition who "will appear as part of the workings of Satan, accompanied by all the power and signs and wonders at the disposal of falsehood." From the second century, scholars have expended much effort trying to identify the Antichrist. Irenaeus, who gives the earliest extensive treatment, identified the Antichrist with Paul's man of lawlessness and the first beast. He expected an unjust king such as a Roman ruler. Polycarp, Tertullian and many others, particularly the Reformers, were inclined to interpret their religious opponents or other heretics as performing the role of Antichrist. While the modern interpretation finds the original meaning in the Roman Empire personified in the evil Nero, one must be cautious about identifying the Antichrist with any subsequent figure. Yet it seems obvious that the Antichrist is a reality in every age.

As in Daniel, the beast can refer not only to an empire but

also to the king who personifies the empire. Irenaeus concluded that the wound must be interpreted in terms of Genesis 3:13f. Christ has wounded Satan and thus freed people from their wound and given them power to wound the beast by overcoming his blasphemy. Everywhere else in the book the word used for wound ("plege") refers to a divinely inflicted plague, judgement, or punishment (9:18). However today there is wide agreement that the wounding of one of the beast's heads (v 3) refers to the legend of *Nero redivivus*. After his suicide in A.D. 68 a rumor spread that in fact Nero had escaped to the East. In contrast with the reputation Nero gained in history, the ordinary people in Rome, and many others in the East who had benefited from his reign, hoped that he would return with the traditional enemies of the Roman Empire, the Parthians, to re-establish his rule over the world. During the period from A.D. 69—88 a number of revolts by people claiming to be Nero took place. Many theories as to the identity of the other six of the seven heads have been proposed. Perhaps the first six are to be interpreted as a selection of the worst, the most hated and feared emperors, such as Caligula, Claudius, Nero, Vespasian, with Domitian as the "one (who) is" and the seventh yet to come.

The beast appears invincible. No one seems able to resist his power, his enticements, his invitation to emperor worship. The question "who can make war against him?" receives the unlikely answer that the only real opposition is provided by the unarmed saints, who eventually did take over the mighty Roman Empire. The question "who is like the beast?" is a parody of the meaning of Michael's name. It recalls the description of the Yahweh of the Exodus found in the triumphant song of the poor Israelites' triumphant escape from

Pharaoh (Ex 15:11; Mic 7:18; Ps 35:10). But the beast is in reality under God's control, and his destructive reign is severely limited. Four times in vv 5-7 the phrase "was given (by God)" is repeated for emphasis. The monster has been given four privileges by the omnipotent God; a blaspheming mouth, authority for a very limited period, a conquest of the holy ones, and universal power.

The reference to blasphemy suggests the claim to divine honours by the emperor. The phrases used recall the epitome of blasphemy against the Most High, the little horn, Antiochus Epiphanes. He also had authority only for a limited period (Dn 7:8ff). The seeming conquest of the holy ones is also based on Daniel 7:21. It means the destruction of their physical bodies as in Matthew 10:28. Likewise in Daniel 3:5f peoples, nations, and languages worship the golden image set up by Nebuchadnezzar. The same words are used in the hymn of praise to the Lamb in 5:9. The worshippers are identified as those not written in the book of life at the world's beginning. Such statements cannot be pressed into a rigid theory of predestination. In 3:5 it was clearly stated that a person's response could cause the removal of their name from the book of life.

This section reaches a climax with an exhortation to listen to these prophetic words and to faithful endurance in the spirit of Jesus. The call to listen was repeated at the end of each of the messages to the seven Churches. The distinctive mark of a Christian is endurance or steadfastness (1:9). Peaceful coexistence with evil is impossible. The difficult verse 10, "If one is destined for captivity . . . if one is destined to be slain by the sword . . ." seems to be a compilation of Jeremiah 15:2; 43:11, and Jesus' saying in Matthew 26:52 ("The one who lives by the sword . . . "). The meaning appears to be that, just as the rebels against God in Jeremiah's day suffered God's punishment, so by contrast the faithful in his day will survive captivity and martyrdom by God's help (cf Phil 1:28). John's endurance is far from allowing oneself to be carried along with the tide of affairs. In contrast to mere resignation it means the courage to face up to life and all it has to offer, with integrity and faith in Jesus, to accept adversity as Jesus accepted the cross and to turn it into glory. In the Jewish world opinions about the Romans varied, from outright collaboration of many Sadducees, to the passive resistance of the Pharisees, to the violent resistance of the Zealots. The Essenes were waiting in the desert for the eschatological battle in which they expected to take a violent part, fighting on God's side. Significantly, John makes no call to violent resistance either now or in the final battle. He implies that faithful endurance through captivity and martyrdom will be a vital contribution to the final defeat of evil.

iv) The Second Beast from the Land, 13:11–18

With the second beast added to the dragon and the first beast, the trinity of evil is complete. The land beast (i.e. from Asia Minor?) is subservient to the cause of the wounded beast from the sea and is later called the false prophet (16:13). Irenaeus, who identified the first beast with a personal Antichrist rather than with Rome, described the second beast as the armour-bearer of the first. Using demonic powers and magic he will deceive the inhabitants of the earth. Hippolytus in the third century described him as the kingdom of the Antichrist. Victorinus in the late third century saw him as the false

prophet who will work magic before the Antichrist. At Pergamum and Thyatira false prophets had already seduced some of
the faithful (2:14f, 20, 24). However, most modern commentators, especially those who see the first beast as *Nero redivivus*,
identify the second beast with the imperial religious establishment. The phrase "two horns like a lamb" suggests that the
beast adopts the attractive guise of the lamb, the symbol of
true religion. However, he speaks "like a dragon," that is, he
boasts and blasphemes (v 5).In Matthew Jesus warned about
false prophets who come in sheep's clothing but inwardly are
savage wolves (Mt 7:15). The beast is described as using the
authority of the first beast to make the whole world worship
it. This may be what John intended, when he mentioned the
false prophets in Pergamum and Thyatira leading the faithful
to idolatry (2:14ff). Luke mentions Asiarchs in Acts 19:31.
These were prominent citizens, friendly to Rome, who over-
saw the various cults, especially that of Emperor worship.
Roman officials saw to it that the local people demonstrated
their allegiance to Rome and could easily employ economic
and other sanctions against those who refused to participate in
the imperial cult. Just as the two witnesses resemble Elijah and
his miracle-working (11:5ff), so also the beast performs great
prodigies and brings fire down from heaven. The Bible consistently insists on the ability of false and deceiving prophets to
work miracles (16:14; 19:20; Dt 13:1ff; Mk 13:22; 2 Thes
2:9). Deception in John means the activity of a false teacher
leading people to worship a false god (2:20). He persuades the
people to make an idol to honour the wounded beast which
lived. Further, he works magic by giving life to the idol. Priests
in the ancient cults used ventriloquism and other deceptions
to animate the idols so that they could make pronouncements

and even move. Just as with the image of Nebuchadnezzar in Daniel 3:1ff, so also now anyone who did not worship the emperor's image was threatened with death.

In 7:1ff we were told that the elect received the protective seal of the living God. In contrast, those who worshipped the imperial idol seem to have received some kind of identifying mark or certificate. "Charagma," the technical term for the imperial stamp, is used. However we have no contemporary evidence to confirm this marking. The marking may be a parody of the Jewish custom of wearing phylacteries on the forehead and the left arm. Obviously, refusal to worship had economic consequences no matter what the social category of the person involved. Significantly, Smyrna was both a poor and a persecuted church (2:9). However, there is no clear evidence that the Romans imposed what we would call economic sanctions against Christians (Rom 15:26; Heb 10:34). The juxtaposition of the image with buying and selling probably alludes to the fact that the currency necessary for buying and selling often carried images of the divine emperor or the goddess Rome. The zealot freedom fighters refused not only to carry but even to look at such images because of their strict interpretation of the command forbiddding the making of images (Ex 20:4).

Identifying the name of the beast with its equivalent number, John now reveals that infamous number to be 666. The translation of the New English Bible is as follows:

Here is the key; and anyone who has intelligence may work out the number of the beast. The number represents a man's name, and the numerical value of its letters is 666.

Interpreters of every age have branded their enemies with this infamous number. It was applied even to the papacy itself by some "spiritual" Franciscans such as Peter John Olivi (1248-1298) and subsequently by different sectarian and reforming movements. Candidates have included Pope Leo X, Martin Luther, Napoleon, Hitler, Stalin, Mussolini, Kissinger, Sadat. It has even been suggested that it is the product code for goods from China, the United States, and several large institutions. Obviously care must be taken with the interpretation to avoid pure subjectivity.

In the ancient world the letters of the Greek and Hebrew alphabets were also used for numbers — alpha and aleph for one, beta and beth for two, etc. The system of adding the numbers symbolised by the letters of a name was known as Gematria. One famous example written on the walls of Pompeii reads: "I love her whose name is 545."

But by Irenaeus' time in the second century the solution was lost. He named three vague names, Euanthos, Teirian, which may refer to the emperor Titus or to the Titans who rebelled against the gods, and Lateinos, which may signify the Roman empire and religious establishment. For Irenaeus, who believed in a personal Antichrist, the number of the beast symbolizes the sum total of all apostate power over six thousand years of injustice, evil deception, and false prophecy. The most popular modern interpretation based on the *Nero redivivus* legend takes the Hebrew consonants for Nero Caesar: N(50), R(200), W(6), N(50), Q(100), S(60), R(200) for a total of 666. However, this would be unintelligible to John's Greek-speaking audience. The Sibylline Oracles (1:328) suggest that Jesus' number is 888, each one better than the perfect 7. Therefore 666 suggests failure upon failure upon failure, and that the reign of evil is thrice doomed. The human state therefore can never be accepted uncritically. It is always far from being perfect, far from divine. No absolute allegiance or reliance should therefore be given to the powers of this world.

v) The Lamb and his Companions on Sion, 14:1–5

In sharp contrast to the vision of the trinity of evil, the dragon and his two beastly minions who are in (deceptive) motion, the Lamb and the elect stand solidly on God's holy Mount Zion (Heb 12:22). In contrast to the beast's followers who bear his mark, the Lamb's followers have his name and the name of his Father on their foreheads. The image seems to be that of the phylactery which, according to Deuteronomy 6:4-5, was worn between the eyes. The writing of the names is the fulfilment of the promise made to the victors at Philadelphia (3:12).

The group at first seems to be identical with those sealed in 7:1-8. But they are described as only the first fruits who have been redeemed from the world.

This vision, which recalls the prophetic descriptions of the day of Yahweh (Joel 2:27), is typical of the author's method of switching frequently from his descriptions of the continuing struggle with evil to giving an encouraging vision of the final triumph. Here we find a new theme which will dominate the final part of the book. The old kingdom symbolized by Zion/Jerusalem is being destroyed and the new is emerging. A certain progress has taken place. In 7:1ff the faithful on earth have been sealed by God for the struggle with evil. In 7:9ff some are already martyred. Now there is a vision of the first fruits of the redeemed with the Lamb in triumph. Mt. Zion was traditionally the place where God or his Messiah would summon the faithful to inaugurate his eschatological reign (Is 24:23; Mic 4:7; Zech 9:9). It is God's resting place where the Messiah is invested with power (Ps 2:6; 90:1ff; 132:13ff).

Next, John hears a sound from heaven which, in a threefold description, he compares to the roaring of many waters (a welcome sound in any hot eastern country), to loud peals of thunder, and to the melody of the temple harpists (1:15; 5:8; 6:1). In contrast to the blasphemous voices of the beast, we have the new victorious song, already sung by the angels for the worthy Lamb (5:9; 7:14-17).

The characteristics of those who alone can learn the new song are fivefold.

(a) They are redeemed from the earth. The verb means bought or purchased (3:18; 5:9). The use here suggests liberation from the power of the beast. But in John's view salvation is clearly the work of the Lamb alone.

(b) "They have never been defiled by immorality with women, for they are virgins" is a statement which has occasioned much comment. Because of the concrete language involved here, some scholars conclude that John means literal celibacy from conversion till death. Both Jesus and Paul clearly praised the virgin lifestyle (1 Cor 7:25ff; Mt 19:12), an option stressed also at Qumran. However, the reference to "defiling" is never used in the New Testament of marriage, which is quite clearly exalted in the New Testament (Heb 13:4; Eph 5:21ff). A literal interpretation leads R.H.Charles to conclude that v 4f, with their male emphasis, are impossible for John and that they were inserted by a misogynist monk arguing for celibacy. Another suggestion sees John portraying the Church in battle array. The reference can be explained in terms of the holy-war regulations for soldiers, who could become ceremonially unclean through sexual relationships (Dt 23:9-10; Lv 15:16; 1 Sam 21:5). However, a metaphorical interpretation seems best. Virgin is a common title for Zion herself in the Old Testament (2 Cor 11:2; 2 Kgs 19:21; Is 23:12; Jer 14:17; Lam 1:15). Idolatry was frequently described as adultery (Ex 34:15; Dt 31:16; Jdg 2:17; Hos 9:1). To practise true religion was to be pure or chaste (2:14). Rome is described as the great harlot in 17:1ff.

(c) In contrast to the whole world which follows the deceptive beast in admiration, "they follow the Lamb wherever he goes." They are obedient to Jesus' call, "Follow Me." In the phrase "wherever he goes" there is a hint of the death of Jesus and a similar martyrdom for the faithful.

(d) They are ransomed (5:9) as the first fruits of humankind for God and the Lamb. Two senses are possible here. The first suggests an untimely death, an initial pledge or sacrifice to God, with more sacrifices to follow (Rom 8:23; 1 Cor 16:15). The general harvest of the faithful is still to follow. A second interpretation recalls the offering of first fruits as a symbol that the whole harvest (now ready) belongs to God. The first fruits or tithes constitute the whole (Jam 1:18; Num 5:9).

(e) No falsehood has been found on their lips, for they are unblemished. Commentators highlight the lack of con-

cern for truth in the modern world and particularly in
some religious establishments. As in Isaiah's description
of the suffering servant (Is 53:9) the meaning may be
that they offered no false prophecies in contrast to the
deceptions of the beast. The word for "unblemished" is
used in the Greek Bible's description of suitable victims
for sacrifice. Thus to accept the deceptions of the beast
would render a person an unsuitable sacrifice to God (1
Pt 1:19).

vi) The Three Angels Announcing Judgement, 14:6–13

The remainder of chapter 14 is unified by a series of angels
who announce the final judgement and carry out the har-
vesting involved. The whole section can be seen as a septet
with three angels at the beginning (v 6-12) and three at the
end (v 14-20), and in the middle John's second beatitude is
emphasised (v 13). The rapid succession of angels is intended
to assure the "blessed" that the triumph of evil in the world
will last for only a brief time, the basic message of the whole
book.

The reference to the first angel as simply "another angel" is
surprising because the last angel mentioned was the angel of
the seventh trumpet in 11:15. The position of the angel flying
in mid-heaven recalls the eagle proclaiming the three "Woes"
(8:13). But this angel is the herald of "eternal good news" to all
humanity — the only place where "Gospel" or "good news"
is used in the whole book. Although the actual content of the
Gospel, which is given, does not contain a specific reference to
Christ, nevertheless it is similar to that given by several
preachers in the early Church (Ac 14:15; 17:24ff; 1 Thes

1:9f). The call to repentance, to fear and worship God the Creator and give him glory, indicates that there is still hope of repentance (Mk 1:15). According to the synoptics, the Gospel would be preached to all the nations before the end would come (Mk 13:10). Everyone will receive the chance to accept the basic Gospel and to acknowledge the Creator before the final judgement. This is the first reference to the judgement in John, although the synonym "wrath" has been found as early as 6:16f.

The judgement theme is taken up in traditional prophetic language by the second angel: "Fallen, fallen is Babylon the great." These words recall Nebuchadnezzar's boast of his self-sufficiency in building Babylon by himself alone, and especially Isaiah's oracle on the fall of Babylon and the destruction of her gods (Is 21:9; Dn 4:30; Gn 11:9). Jewish sources used such names as Edom, Egypt, and Babylon to symbolise Rome. But the choice Babylon was particularly suitable because, like Rome, Babylon also destroyed the temple and Jerusalem. The story of Jeremiah, Jerusalem, the Temple, and the Babylonians provides an amazing parallel to the story of Jesus, Jerusalem, the Temple, and the Romans. The mention of the fall of Babylon, the symbol of evil, at this point is an interesting example of John's lack of chronological order. The actual fall will be described only with the final bowl judgement, 16:9ff. The reason given for the fall of Babylon is the seductive influence of her corrupt ways. Like a temple prostitute she intoxicates her victims before seducing them (51:7f).

The third angel (v 9-12) gives a blunt warning against compromise by luridly painting the disastrous consequences which are inevitable. To drink the wine of Babylon is equivalent to drinking the wine of God's "passionate" wrath, as the special word for wrath indicates. This is a lurid passage and one of the clearest in the New Testament on the unending suffering in hell. It would be very attractive to consider such passages as unchristian and to remove them from our exposition of Christian doctrine. But as C. S. Lewis points out in *The Problem of Pain*, the important question is whether the doctrine is true. He insists that the doctrine has the full support of Jesus' own teaching, that it has always been held by Christians, and that it has the support of reason. Contrary to some interpreters there is no vindictive gloating here over the prospective torture of sinners. Rather, the grim passage is written as a deterrent for Christians. The passage is a call to patient endurance, to obedience to God's commands (Jn 6:29), and to the faith of Jesus — a rare reference to the "historical" Jesus!

In sharp contrast to the punishment of the wicked, an encouraging voice from heaven now pronounces blessed those who die in the Lord (1:3; 1 Cor 15:18). Further, the Spirit, who speaks only rarely in this book (2:7, 11ff; 22:17), solemnly adds that "they will find rest from their labours because their good works will follow them" (2:2; 20:12f). This was a traditional Jewish teaching found in the Pirke Aboth (6:9), the Sayings of the Fathers:

> At the hour when a man dies neither silver nor gold nor precious stones or pearls accompany him, but Torah (obedience to the commandments) and good works.

According to Adela Yarbro Collins, the messages of the three angels are still relevant today. The commands to fear God and

worship him remind us of the limited and relative character of
our views, the deep reverence for the invisible origin of all
things, the fragility of our existence and its character as gift,
the danger of an unbalanced attachment to any transient
manifestations, and our accountability for our deeds, however
that will take place. Like the beast from the sea, Babylon
symbolises counterfeit power, and her doom exposes the
futility of the will to a power which ultimately destroys those
who exercise or submit to it. The blessed are those who resist
the will to power and are faithful to the source of all things.
For them death is truly rest.

(vii) The Harvest of the Earth, 14:14–20

The first fruits of the harvest were mentioned in 14:4, followed by three angels announcing judgement. Now the
climax has arrived and is described in terms quite familiar to
those with an agricultural background: the grain harvest and
the grape harvest. Or rather, the end has almost arrived! With
his typical delaying technique, John has stopped the action
since the blowing of the seventh trumpet in 11:15 to focus on
the two rivals for world dominion: the dragon and the Lamb.
Now the pace will increase somewhat as he describes the
seven last plagues in chapters 15-16 and then the final
destruction of the beast and Babylon in chapters 17-19.

In 1:7 Jesus was described as about to come upon the
clouds. Now John sees a "son of man" (i.e., a human figure in
contrast to the beastly figure) with a crown of gold and a sharp
sickle, sitting on a white cloud (1:13). However, there is some
doubt that Christ is meant because the following v 17 refers to
"another" angel. The descriptive phrase "like a son of man"

seems to be used of angels in Daniel 8:16; 10:16. The image of the harvest is used in Jeremiah 51:33 for the divine judgement on Babylon. The judgement symbols of sickle, grain harvest and vintage are found in Joel 3:13 (Hos 6:11). Jesus also used the harvest image (Mt 13:39; Jn 4:35) and the vineyard as a symbol of Israel (Mk 12:1ff).

The image of the grape harvest seems to be drawn from Isaiah 63:3, where an angry God takes vengeance on Edom like one treading the "press for vines" until their blood spurts on his garments. Significantly, it is another angel (v 17) and not the son of man who implements the vintage of God's anger. The fact that the winepress is trodden "outside the city" is perhaps an allusion to the fate of Jesus. He was crucified outside the city and his blood flowed from his side (Jn 19:20ff; Heb 13:12-14). Perhaps the city of God, the place of refuge, is meant. Another explanation draws on the Jewish tradition that the final battle was to be fought near Jerusalem (Dn 11:45; Joel 4:2). The battle will be so terrible that it will result in a sea of blood as high as a horse's bridle stretching for nearly two hundred miles. Traditional hyperbolic language is apparently involved here. 1 Enoch (100:1-3) describes men killing one another until their horses walk up to the breast in the blood of sinners. The number may be a rough estimate of the length of Palestine, and the blood bath the result of a gradual invasion such as the one before the Roman destruction of the Temple. Palestine was very familiar with the bloodbaths caused by successive power-hungry empires. Another suggestion is that the number is the product of the square of four, the earth's number multiplied by the square of ten to signify the complete harvest and judgement of the whole earth.

This theme of wrath and anger disturbs many. Yet, to separate wrath from love is impossible because wrath and love

properly understood are not enemies but essential comple-
ments, however much in tension they may co-exist. Love
alone can so easily become naive, sentimental folly or even
permissive tolerance. Wrath and its biblical synonym, justice,
can easily become cold, severe, inhuman, calculating, ultimately diabolical, and a burden to the weak. Both are needed.
Yet to hold two such disparate emotions and ideas at the same
time and still retain the ability to function is almost impossible
for a human being. According to F. Scott Fitzgerald it is the
sign of a first-rate intelligence and runs contrary to the
common tendency to believe in clear-cut solutions. If John
overstresses the wrath aspect his message is all too necessary in
our overly permissive society. A key function of prophecy is to
attempt to right the balance by stressing, and perhaps over-
stressing, the neglected element of the life-giving polarity.

One can trace a certain development in the biblical understanding of God's wrath. Before the Exile, when Yahweh was
seen as the personal God of Israel, Yahweh's wrath was
described as personal and directed mainly against Israel itself.
In the post-exilic time the prophets again emphasise the
personal dimension, but its object is as much the Gentiles as
the faithless Jews. The eschatological dimension also becomes
prominent. These aspects are evident in Ezekiel who had a
strong influence on John and who stresses God's anger more
than any other Old Testament writer. But with writers such as
Daniel, and the authors of Psalms and Proverbs, the idea of
anger becomes more impersonal, somewhat akin to an inevitable process in history. Before the New Testament period two
further aspects of the divine anger are emphasised: that it can
be disciplinary and that the death of an innocent can appease
the divine anger.

(5) THE SEVEN LAST PLAGUES, 15:1–16:21

The opening verses which emphasise the completion or accomplishment of the wrath of God provide a fitting climax to what has gone before (6:17; 11:14) and an introduction to the seven last plagues (ch 16) and the fall of Babylon (ch 17-18). Before describing the woes of the seven trumpets, John highlighted the protective sealing of the faithful (8:1ff). Now, before telling about the final seven plagues, he again anticipates the final victorious song of the faithful.

John sees another sign or portent. He has already seen in heaven a human sign, the woman representing the faithful, and a diabolic sign, the dragon.

Now he sees a "great and wonderful" sign. The word "wonderful" is not normally used of human persons and affairs, but for what is divine. Seven angels hold the seven last plagues. The word "plague" was used of misfortune in general in the Old Testament. But it was used in particular for the last plague in Egypt, the death of the first born; of the suffering servant; and the blows suffered by the man on the road to Jericho (Ex 11:1-9; Is 53:3; Lk 10:30). In a sense, the account of the seven plagues tells nothing new. Rather it goes over the same old story in typical Oriental style of repetition with new symbolism and new details. The eschatological judgement has already been described under the three symbols of the cup of wine (14:10), the grain harvest (14:14-16), and the vintage (14:17-20).

Many details of the description in chapter 15 show that there is an Exodus background in John's mind: the plagues, the sea, the Song of Moses, the tent of witness, the destruction of the persecutors. Other New Testament writers such as Paul also described the Christian life as a new Exodus (1 Cor 5:7;

10:1ff; 2 Cor 3:6). The Exodus experience was particularly appropriate, for it led to the discovery that God was not on the side of the Pharaohs and Empires of the day but on the side of the rabble or "riffraff" (Num 11:4-6). The real liberation of the Jewish people to worship and serve one God alone took place on Mt. Sinai where they became a priestly and kingly people, a theme dear to John (1:6).

John has described the image of the sea of glass in 4:6 but now it is "mingled with fire." This unusal image suggests the fire through which the martyrs have passed, or the wrath to fall on the world, or perhaps the Red Sea which has been safely crossed. Standing solidly on the sea are those who had conquered the beast of chaos, his image and his numbers. Just as Jesus' crucifixion was his rising in triumph, so martyrdom was seen in the early Church as victory, as one's birthday and the beginning of the new heavenly life. According to William Barclay the real victory is "not to live in safety, to evade trouble, cautiously and prudently to preserve life; the real victory is to face the worst that evil can do, and, if need be, to be faithful unto death."

John hears the victors singing with God-given harps. Just as the Hebrews sang their song of freedom after escaping from Egypt so now the victors sing "the song of Moses the servant of God, and the song of the Lamb." The ancient song of Moses has become the song of the Lamb who now offers true and ultimate liberation to all nations. Nearly every phrase of this song can be found some place in the Old Testament (Ps 11:2; 139:14; 86:8f; Mal 1:11). The song is addressed to God rather than to the Lamb and is closer to the Song of Moses found in Dt 32 than to the triumphant version found in Ex 15. There is no note of self-congratulation or self-importance. All is of God.

It is a song of hope for the conversion of the nations. None will be able to resist the righteous or saving acts of the one God who alone is holy. Power, justice, truth, holiness are his qualities.

Next, an even more impressive vision is described (v 5-8) as the door to heaven's temple is again opened (11:19). Now the image is not Solomon's temple but its prototype, the tent of witness which was the shelter for the ark in the desert. There Moses went to meet God and to receive God's revelation and message. In Maccabees 2:4ff the tent was expected to appear in the messianic days when God will gather *his* people and show them *his* mercy.

Seven angels dressed in white and gold, symbols of purity, priesthood and royalty, come forth. Each is given a "bowl filled with the wrath of God who lives for ever and ever." In 5:8 the golden bowls were described as containing the prayers of the faithful. Bowls were used for drinking, for ointment, and for incense in the temple. Jeremiah was commanded to take a cup of the wine of God's wrath and make the kingdoms of the world and especially the king of Babylon drink and become crazy (Jer 25:15-26). The smoke that filled the temple symbolised God's special and awesome presence. Cloud and smoke prevented Moses from entering the tent in Exodus 40:5. A similar occurrence takes place at key points in Jewish history (Is 6:4; Ezek 10:3f; 1 Kg 8:10-14; 2 Chr 7:2f). John, drawing on such tremendous scenes of God's presence, insists that no one can enter until after the inevitable and final plagues. God is so powerful and so unapproachable that nothing can withstand his final judgment.

The Seven Bowls of Wrath, 16:1–21

It is almost impossible to speak adequately in human terms of the wrath and justice of the mysterious Yahweh. John adapts into his sevenfold model the imagery available to him from his traditions, especially the Old Testament plagues, the teaching of the Exodus that Yahweh was good news to the oppressed. His purpose is to give hope to his small communities who are so politically powerless in the face of the colossus of Rome. The Roman war machine so easily ground small nations into the dust. To be labelled a protestor or to opt out of the official cult of the Roman state with its increasingly totalitarian demands could easily lead to economic, religious, and even tragic consequences. John insists that God is no capricious, cruel dictator. His justice is based on the responsibility of each person for the consequences of their actions. John is concerned to provide an answer to the relevant question "Who is like the beast and who can fight against it?" (13:4). His answer is the Christian community.

There is an obvious comparison between the trumpet and bowl sequences which shows that the author is going over the same material again. In the second of each sequence the sea turns to blood, in the third the rivers and fountains turn to blood, in the sixth both have the Euphrates River, and in the seventh there is lightning, voices, thunder, earthquakes and hail. However, in comparison to the effects of the seals and trumpets there is an air of finality and increasing intensity among the quickly moving series of bowl plagues. The seals affect a quarter of the earth and the trumpets a third, but the destruction of the bowls is total (6:8; 8:7ff). In the first four trumpets, as in the first five plagues in Egypt, there is no direct suffering inflicted on people. But in the bowls people are attacked from the very beginning. Likewise the traditional areas of nature, the earth, sea, fresh water, and planets are affected. Theologically there is little that is new. However, the emphasis is more clearly directed against unrepentant Rome and its emperor worship, thus preparing for the definitive judgement in the following chapters.

The word used for sores in the first plague is also found in the description of the sickness of Job, Hezekiah, and Lazarus (Job 2:7; 2 Kgs 20:7; Lk 16:21). It recalls the sixth plague of boils in Exodus 9:9ff. Just as the enemies of Moses were stricken, so those who had the mark of the beast and worship his image are stricken. The fact that the faithful are preserved suggests that the plagues should not be interpreted literally. The message is that evil leads to suffering, punishment, and God's judgement. The voice which calls them forth from the inaccessible tent is probably that of God himself.

In the second bowl, the sea, the dragon's base, is corrupted "like the blood of a dead person" so that every creature in it dies. This is the reversal of the creative act in Genesis 1:21 and recalls Moses' first plague when he turned the waters of Egypt to blood (Ex 7:14ff). The third plague intensifies the third trumpet's effects. There a third of the waters becomes bitter (8:10f). Now all the earth's water is turned into blood. The thought of drinking blood instead of water was particularly obnoxious to the Hebrew mentality (Lv 17:10). Perhaps there is an allusion to the battle on Lake Gennesareth during the Roman invasion. According to Josephus, after the Roman naval victory "the whole lake was red with blood and covered with corpses, for not a man escaped" (War 3:522ff).

The angel of the waters and even the altar insist that God's punishment and judgement of those who shed the blood of the saints and prophets, are just (cf 15:3f). To have their drinking water changed into blood is their proper desert. The reference to the "angel of the waters" and the speaking altar may be mere personification. However, John has already spoken of angels of the winds and an angel of fire (7:1; 14:18) in accordance with the Jewish tradition which assigned to the angels various spheres of influence. The voice from the altar recalls the souls of the martyrs crying out for justice under the altar (6:9).

The punishment "which fits the crime" is not a final retaliation but is remedial in purpose because it is intended to lead to repentance and to give God glory (v 9). The choice, and it is a real choice that John places before his audience, is to shed the blood of the saints and to drink blood, or to wear garments dipped in the blood of the Lamb. Paul made the same point in Galatians 6:7, when he insisted that no one makes a fool of God but rather "one will reap only what one sows." G. B. Caird in his commentary suggests that John is drawing on The Book of Wisdom (C.B.C. 100). In this book he finds three important principles at the base of God's direction of history: God's use of creation to requite his enemies (5:17), the punishment of a person by the very things through which one sins (11:16), and the benefiting of those in need by the things through which their foes were punished (11:5).

The fourth plague of the scorching sun, evidently aimed only at unbelievers, is the reverse of the protection from the sun provided to those washed in the blood of the Lamb (7:16). Instead of the typical apocalyptic darkening of the sun (8:12) the sun actually flares up in intensity to burn people with fire.

A Jewish midrash comments that just as the sun burned up Esau but healed Jacob so it will heal the just descendant of Jacob and burn up the pagan idolators. The result is in sharp contrast with the activity of the two witnesses in 11:13 where disasters lead to the conversion of the rest. Instead they blaspheme the name of God (13:6), an accusation repeated in the fifth plague.

The fifth plague recalls the darkening of the fifth seal (9:2) and the ninth plague in Egypt (Ex 10:21-23). This darkness poured on the throne of the beast is best taken symbolically for mental and spiritual blindness. It suggests the political chaos which took place in Rome with the suicide of Nero. According to Is 8:19-22, darkness and gloom follow the consultation of mediums and fortune tellers. Instead of conversion they cursed God and "gnawed their tongues for pain." The rare word "gnaw" is found again only in Job 30:3 where Job describes what a disdainful lot are those who deride him.

The sixth bowl plague (vv 12-16) with its reference to Armageddon is one of the most famous passages in the book. The first result is the drying up of the river Euphrates so that the kings of the East can advance on Babylon. Cyrus the Great had damned the river to capture the city in the sixth century B.C. (according to Herodotus, 1:191). The ironical reference recalls the stopping of the waters of the Red Sea and the Jordan to enable the Hebrews to cross in safety (Ex 14:21; Josh 3:17). Similar miracles worked for, not against, the Hebrews were expected in the future (Is 11:15f; Jer 51:36; Zech 10:10-12). There is a striking similarity to the sixth trumpet plague and the release of the demonic hordes to invade Israel (9:14). Here the result is to prepare the assembly of the mysterious rulers of the East to do battle with the Almighty Yahweh. But curiously, they are not mentioned again.

Behind the unholy war lie the dragon and the beast, and the beast from the earth with the new title of the false prophet. Together they form an unholy triumvirate and resemble the deceiving spirit which enticed Ahab into battle (1 Kgs 22:21ff). Three times emphasising the word "mouth," perhaps with the sense of command, John imagines the emergence of three froglike hostile forces. To characterise the dirty activity of the unholy trinity and its wonder-working (13:13), John could hardly have picked a more revolting image than the unclean frog which was associated with the second plague in Egypt (Ex 7:25ff; Lev 11:10, 41).

For the Persians the frog was the double of Ahriman the god of evil and the agent of plagues. For the Egyptians the frog was a symbol of Hegt the goddess of fertility and resurrection. But such symbolism was a form of idolatry for the Jewish people and an indication of demonic influence (9:20; 1 Cor 10:20f). Slimy and ugly with their useless and ceaseless croaking, frogs provided a devastating caricature of the evil monsters which the early Christian feared, the demonic influence of the state and its fawning sycophants.

Rather abruptly in the midst of the gathering of the evil forces for the great day of battle, Jesus himself appears. He issues a warning to the community that he comes like a thief and pronounces the book's third beatitude on those who watch. The prophetic warning about the second coming recalls the warnings to Sardis and Laodicea (3:2, 18) and has many parallels in the New Testament (Mt 24:43; Lk 12:39; 1 Th 5:2; 2 Pt 3:10). In particular this warning shows that there is no possibility of decoding Jesus' words to discover the date of Armageddon. Nevertheless during the history of the Church various adventist groups have succumbed to the human temptation to construct detailed timetables for the end of the world, e.g. 1914, 1959, 1990, 2000. Such a warning also demonstrates that John's aim is not to give detailed historical and geographical information. Like an ancient prophet he knows no more than his audience about such matters, but he is concerned to appeal to their consciences. Watchfulness means keeping their garments (on or ready?) like a soldier ready for duty. Nakedness was abhorrent to the Jews. It symbolised lack of spiritual preparation (3:18).

Then John suddenly switches back to describe the gathering together of the kings in the place "called in Hebrew 'Armageddon'" (v 16). No such place is found on any map of the ancient world, nor is it mentioned in the Old Testament. The word may mean "city of Megiddo", or if one prefixes an "H", "mountain of Megiddo." Some two hundred battles were fought near Megiddo to make it an appropriate symbol for the final battle with evil in which God wins not with armies but by his incarnate word Jesus (2 Kgs 23:29; Zech 12:11; 17:14). In John's day it was a mere "tell" or mound some 70 feet high.

Megiddo, one of the fortress cities of Solomon, stood at a key pass between the coastal plains of Palestine and the interior plain of Esdraelon. Armies from Egypt and Asia passed through to do battle with one another. There, when Israel had neither shield nor spear, the Lord helped Deborah rout Sisera and his 900 chariots of iron in what became a highly symbolic victory over evil (Jdg 5:19). Other possible translations are "his fruitful mountain" or "mount of assembly" or "city of desire," i.e. Jerusalem (Joel 3:2), or "destroying mountain" (Jer 51:25). There is perhaps an allusion to the last battle with Gog and Magog which Ezekiel placed in the mountains of Israel (Ezek 38:8ff). John's point is that ultimately evil will be destroyed no matter how powerful it may seem.

The long seventh bowl plague (vv 17-21), which resembles the third woe (11:14-19), is the climax and opens the way for the elaborate description of the fall of Babylon/Rome and the final judgement in the following chapters. This bowl is poured "into the air" (Wis 7:3). Perhaps this vague reference means into the abode of demons (9:2). Or, because all people and life depend on air, the symbolism suggests a universal destruction. John's emphasis is to give God's interpretation from the temple: "It is done" or "It has come to pass," a Greek verb which is found again in 21:6 (11:15) to describe how the eternal God makes all things new. Just when one perhaps expects something different, John again surprises us with a tremendous theophany which seems to recall the destruction of Jerusalem by Titus in A.D. 70. The unprecedented earthquake splits the great city into three parts. The allusion seems to be to the three factions, led by Simon bar Giora, Eleazar the Zealot, and John of Gischala, who were busy fighting one another in the besieged city. The historian Josephus (War 5:1ff) suggests that this was the result of divine justice. John's view is that the same kind of destruction will befall the Romans as they themselves wreaked on Jerusalem. His message is that God remembers and that Babylon will drink the cup of his anger (14:8ff). The destruction of Babylon is imagined in typical apocalyptic style. Islands and mountains disappear, and a fantastic plague of hundredweight hailstones rains down on people (6:14; Zech 14:10). The hail recalls the seventh plague in Egypt (Ex 9:23f; Josh 10:11) as well as the gigantic stones hurled by the Roman catapults against their enemies. Unfortunately, instead of repentance, the result is that God is blasphemed. The stage is now set for John's description of the fall of Rome and God's final triumph.

E. The Verdict on the Great Harlot, 17:1–18:24

Chapters 17 and 18 describe the verdict on Babylon announced in 16:19. Chapter 17 begins with a vision of the great harlot and the beast which she rides (v 1-6), then gives an interpretation of the vision (vv 7-18). Chapter 18 describes dreadful ruin in images drawn from the Old Testament accounts of the destruction of famous cities. This description leads into chapter 19 which shows the heavenly joy over the conquest of evil.

The vision opens with one of the seven angels, who hold the seven bowls, thus establishing a loose connection with the previous judgement scenes. John is shown a "great prostitute who is established on many waters." Because non-Jewish religious worship frequently involved sacred prostitution, words such as prostitute and prostitution were particularly apt to describe false religion in Jewish eyes. The figure of a harlot city is used in Nahum 3:4 of Nineveh and of Babylon in Jeremiah 51. In Isaiah 23:17, which is perhaps the background here, the wealth and commerce of Tyre is described as the fee paid to a prostitute. Jerusalem itself is described as a harlot in Ezekiel 16 and 23. All these cities have certain aspects in common such as kingly splendour, abundant prosperity and even luxury, self-confidence and pride, oppression, violence, and injustice against God's people. Jeremiah had described Babylon as sitting on many waters, probably referring to its abundant commerce from its many canals and waterways. The sin of the great prostitute was the corruption of the Mediterranean world and its leaders with its values, its power-seeking, its violence, and its false religion.

John is carried into the desert where, free from the charms

of Roman civilization, he can get a proper view of the nature of the Roman Empire and its seductions. His image is rather comic, a gaudy prostitute riding on a revolting dragon. The adornment of the woman in purple and scarlet, glittering gold and jewels and pearls indicates a life-style of unlimited luxury. But her golden cup is filled "with the disgusting filth of her abominations." Some of these have been spelled out in chapter 13 in the description of the beast as a parody of Jesus, with its hollow power, its self-centered lust to dominate others, its false understanding of its place in the universe.

As was the custom of Roman prostitutes, the prostitute's name was on a headband on her forehead (Jer 3:3), "a mystery, Babylon the great, the mother of prostitutes." The use of the word mystery (1:20) suggests that the name Babylon needs a further interpretation, given in v 7ff. This mother prostitute, who is called Babylon, is the mother of all the idolatry on the earth. Therefore one cannot simply say that she is ancient Babylon, Jerusalem, or Rome, but rather that she is the source of all their wickedness and, in particular, the killing of the martyrs of Jesus. Martyrs normally means a witness to Jesus. This is the beginning of its use for one who dies so as to witness to Jesus (6:9; 12:11). To be drunk with blood symbolized the lust for violence in the ancient world.

Most commentators agree that for John Babylon was a symbolic name for Rome, a city and empire which, for him was the incarnation and source of evil. In the rabbinic writings other symbolic names were frequent such as Egypt, Kittim, and the most common of all, Edom. But he probably selected Babylon because it most resembled Rome which also destroyed Jerusalem and its temple. Both also were symbols of wealth, great power, and decadence. It is highly unlikely that any non-Christian would not have penetrated the symbolism here as it was so obvious. Therefore its purpose was not to conceal the allusions to Rome, such as the seven hills, but to use what Adela Yarbro Collins calls the "intrinsic evocative power" of symbolism in writing to the Christian community. Certainly John's hyperbolic view of Roman power is an educative caricature. But a reading of Barclay's commentary shows that Roman writers themselves are far more unrestrained by comparison. Seneca described Rome as "a filthy sewer." Perhaps behind John's description of the great prostitute lies Claudius' wife Messalina who, according to Juvenal and Tacitus, regularly served as a prostitute in a common brothel until the emperor had her put to death.

John, who was invited to see a verdict, instead sees a magnificent-looking harlot and so "wondered with a great wonder." As in 7:13ff, an angel gives an interpretation first of the beast (v 7-8), then the seven heads (v 9-11), the ten horns (v 12-14), the waters (v 15), the woman (v 18). The words, "Here is the clue for one who possesses wisdom" (v 9), show that the meaning is not all that obvious. Even a rapid survey of scholars' interpretations confirms this point. However the final verse, "The woman is the great city which has sovereignty over the kings of the earth," seems to be a clear reference to Rome as is also the reference to the seven hills which was frequent in Roman writers. The description of the beast in v 7-8 is the same as that in 13:1ff and probably alludes to the legend that Nero, the first emperor to persecute Christians, was coming back to life probably in the person of Domitian. The book of life was also mentioned in 13:8.

However, the difficult sentence v 9-11, which suggests that five emperors have fallen while a sixth is reigning and a seventh is yet to come, has provoked many interpretations and no clear-cut solution. Perhaps John is referring to his contemporary Domitian, the "one (who) is," having selected five of the most odious emperors (Caligula, Claudius, Nero, Vespasian, Titus) to make up the six of the traditional number seven. The eighth would really be one of the seven because Nero has come back to life. The prediction of a short reign for the last emperor shows the intense expectation of the end which characterises the whole book.

The ten horns (v 12-14) are explained as ten kings, who have not yet come to power, but who will reign only for a very short time — one hour. Strong animals fought and pushed with their horns. Horns became symbols for political power and for kings (Dn 7:8ff; Ps 132:17). These have been variously interpreted as earthly kings or governors of Roman provinces or demonic powers. Perhaps they should be interpreted symbolically as an indefinite number representing those who offer their service to the political power Rome to persecute the faithful. For a time they will ally with the beast to fight the Lamb but "the Lamb will conquer them." Two reasons for victory are given. The Lamb, not the earthly rulers, is the real Lord of Lords and King of Kings. Secondly, his followers are "called chosen and faithful" (Mt 22:14) in contrast to the followers of the prostitute. Despite her multitudes of followers the kings will turn against the prostitute in hatred, strip her of her finery, devour her and set her on fire like the punishment of the prostitute Oholibah (Ezek 23:25ff). Thus John paints a vivid picture of the self-destruction of evil, of the fickleness of human alliances, of the hollowness of any system which does not worship the one true God. One after another Egypt, Assyria, Babylon, Persia, Greece, Rome, Portugal, Spain, Germany, France, Britain, Japan have built empires with the wrong kind of power, with arrogant egoism and a confidence that they would last for ever. But all have fallen. For John, all is under God's control. He follows the Old Testament view that God can even use evil powers to punish Israel, to work unto an ultimate good (Jer 25:9-14; Lk 20:18). Nothing can stop his decree (10:3). The same word "gnome" is used in Daniel for the edicts of the Persian kings. Therefore one can already sing a lament and write an anticipatory obituary for Babylon (not the end of the whole world!) as the writer proceeds to do in chapter 18. Amos sang a similar lamentation before the fall of Israel:

> Fallen, no more to rise,
> is the virgin Israel;
> forsaken on her land,
> with none to raise her up (Am 5:2)

This chapter 18 is almost all poetry, written in the spirit of the prophetic doom songs and in particular Ezekiel's description of the fall of the prince of Tyre (Ezek 28). The fact that apart from the word "apostles" in v 20 there is no distinctively Christian emphasis has led a number of commentators to suggest that the writer is using an earlier Jewish document. But even if this is so, the wider context of the author's reflection on the coming of Christ has transformed its meaning. Like a Greek tragic dramatist the writer does not directly describe the fall of Babylon, but rather, with some of the most beautifully cadenced language in the whole book, he is content to record a variety of chorus-like reactions to the disaster. He begins with an angel proclaiming a dirge of judgement (18:1-

3) followed by a command to God's people to leave the
doomed city (v 4-8). Then he gives a series of three more
dirges or laments from the kings of the earth (v 9-10), the
merchants (v 11-17), and the sea captains (v 18-20). The
chapter finishes as it began with a vision of an angel and a
repeated dirge proclaiming judgement and doom (v 21-24).

The chapter opens with the coming of another angel from
heaven (10:1) with great authority and a glory which filled the
earth with light. This picture which recalls Ezekiel's description of the Shekinah returning to the Temple (Ezek 43:2)
contrasts with the hollow authority of the scarlet woman in
the previous scenes. In words which recall the prophetic
condemnation of ancient Babylon, the total destruction and
abandonment of the city is proclaimed (Is 13:19ff). It will
become a place for demons, for every kind of foul spirit and
hateful birds. Three charges are given as reasons for this awful
destruction; Babylon's corruptive influence on all nations, the
fact that the (minor) kings of the earth committed fornication
with her (17:2), and "the merchants of the earth have grown
rich from her wealth and wantonness." Economic historians
have observed that the situation in Asia Minor from Vespasian's rule to that of Hadrian was one of social unrest and
continuous tension between rich and poor. Luxury-loving
Rome created an economic boom in which merchants grew
rich at the expense of the ordinary people of the Roman world.
John is not envious of the rich or of riches as such. Rather he is
against exploitation by the Babylons of our world.

The heavenly call "come out of her, my people," which
concludes with the words, "God has remembered her iniqui-
ties," seems to come from God. This call to "come out" is
found often in the Bible from Abraham onward and recalls in

particular the Exodus motif (Gn 12:1; Jer 50:8). It should not be interpreted as a mere piece of advice to leave the city. Rather, it is a warning to the faithful against succumbing to the temptations of the luxury-loving, comfortable Roman values and lifestyle. Already in chapters 2-3 John has warned his communities against the deceits and snares of a life of compromise. That sin inevitably leads to plagues and punishment is the message and warning which the voice gives. "God remembers" is a sombre warning. Then the voice commands that the punishment fit the crimes of Babylon: "Render to her as she has rendered" (v 6). John is probably alluding to Rome's destruction of Jerusalem and Nero's persecution of the Christians. Three reasons are given for Babylon's punishment: her wanton self-glorification, her boasting that she was a self-sufficient queen in command even of the future (Is 47:7ff), and her claim that she would never be a mourning widow. Because she seems to forget that God is a mighty judge she will suddenly, "in one day," experience what her luxurious lifestyle made her forget, the four plagues of death, mourning, famine, and fire. The "burning with fire" recalls the common practice of burning cities to the ground. In Judaism burning was the punishment for harlotry if the adulteress was a priest's daughter (Lv 21:9). One method was to pour molten lead down a person's throat.

Next, John, drawing on Ezekiel 27, describes how allied kings, merchants, sea captains, and sailors mourn Babylon's catastrophe. Each of the three lamentations ends with the repeated "Woe, woe." Opinions vary among writers as to John's view of the catastrophe. D. H. Lawrence's view that such passages express the envy of the "haves" and "have-nots" is too superficial a reading of modern psychology into John.

Writers like Swete seem far too extreme with such comments as "with a touch of grim humour, he paints them standing at a safe distance from the conflagration, and contenting themselves with idle lamentations." Certainly the book rejoices in the triumphs of God's justice. The three laments provide a human touch in the midst of the pronouncements of doom. Further, a sympathetic reading seems to indicate some appreciation of the beauty, culture, and greatness of Rome and her civilization despite the economic hardships which it inflicted on so many.

The dirge of the kings seems to express the genuine lament of Rome's friends for the sudden collapse of "Babylon the mighty." However, they keep their distance for fear lest they share her suffering since they had "wallowed in her sensuality." Anyone who had doubts about the unbelievable sensuality of Rome should read Barclay's commentary and the quotations he gives from contemporary writers.

The second and central lament comes from the merchants of the world who will have no more market for their imports. The Talmud remarks that Rome cornered nine-tenths of the wealth of the world, leaving only one-tenth for the rest. The merchants' mourning is not due to any friendship or patriotic motives or care for the suffering but is based on greed because "this great wealth has been destroyed." In a catalogue reminiscent of Ezekiel 27, John lists twenty-eight different imports like a description of an exotic bazaar, to demonstrate the proverbial luxury of Rome. Significantly, he ends his list with a phrase which translates "slaves, that is, human beings." Rome was an empire based on slavery, on the exploitation and degradation of unfortunate human beings. In like manner, all world empires throughout history have engaged in the exploitation of people.

3.   The third lament (v 17-20) comes from the captains, the sailors, and those who travel the sea. Their mourning, though loss of profits is involved, seems more sincere because in traditional biblical fashion they throw dust on their heads, a sign of humility and lowliness (Job 2:12; Ezek 27:30). Their cry of admiration, "What city could have been compared with this great one?" echoes the cry of those who worshipped the dragon and the beast (13:4).

The threefold lament is abruptly interrupted by an appeal to the heavens, the saints, apostles, and prophets to rejoice not precisely that Babylon has fallen but because God has pronounced judgement against her for you. This type of call disturbs some critics who forget the real suffering situation being described. Rather, the text is in the spirit of the Magnificat and expresses a passionate trust in God's justice, not a vindictive outcry or envious outburst. Apart from the reference to false apostles in 2:2 this is almost the only reference to apostles in the book (21:14). Perhaps the allusion is to the martyrdom of James by Herod and that of Peter and Paul by Nero (Ac 12:1-2).

The final and rather poignant lament begins with a mighty angel symbolically hurling a stone, as big as a huge millstone, into the sea. Jeremiah had also used the figure of a stone cast into the Euphrates to symbolise the fall of Babylon (Jer 51:63). The angel explains the symbolism of the stone — Babylon will likewise disappear forever in four terms: violence, forever, silence, and darkness. He gives a melancholy list of what will no longer be found in Babylon: all kinds of music, crafts, grinding of corn, the lighting of lamps, the joy of marriage. Babylon will be as desolate as fallen Jerusalem (Jer 25:10). Two reasons for the disaster bring the chapter to a sorrowful conclusion. Babylon's merchants were the world's great people but they had led astray all the nations with their magic spells (9:21). Economic gain was their only goal. Further, Babylon was responsible for the deaths of the prophets and saints and "all who were slain on the earth" (17:6). This is a clear indication that the city of Babylon is just a symbol of the violence which pervades the whole earth for all time, a violence which will be redressed (Mt 23:35).

F. Alleluia — Victory — the Lamb's Wedding, 19:1-10

In contrast to the laments of Babylon's associates, chapter 19 begins with a series of alleluias and songs of praise, leading up to the coming of the faithful and true rider of the white horse (v 11). This is the climax of the seven bowls cycle.

The first alleluia is in answer to the call of 18:20 "rejoice over her, you heavens." This alleluia sounds like the loud cry of a great multitude in heaven. The word alleluia, so familiar in our hymns, was frequently used to introduce or conclude a Psalm. It gave the name Hallel to Psalms 113-118, the group of Psalms which Jesus and the disciples sang at the end of the Last Supper (Mt 26:30). Such psalms were important at Jewish feasts as a joyful reminder of God's past triumphs and a source of confidence for the future. The word derives from "hallel," to praise, and "Yah" for Yahweh. The aim of such hymns is simply to invite praise for God and to develop some of the motives for such praise. It insists that salvation (victory), glory, and power (4:11; 12:10) belong to our God and not to any human empire or achievement. No mere "spiritual" salvation is meant here but rather all dimensions of it are intended from material to political to spiritual. Three reasons are given: God's judgements are true and just, as the altar cried out in 16:7; God has judged the great harlot which corrupted the earth, as the angel had promised in 17:1; and God has avenged the blood of his servants which she had shed (6:9ff).

The second alleluia (v 3) celebrates the permanent destruction of evil Babylon in words which recall Isaiah's judgement: "its smoke will go up for ever" (Is 34:9f). In response, the twenty-four elders and the four living creatures, in their last appearance in the book, proclaim their joyful approval "Amen" (4:9f). Then a voice from the throne exhorts all God's servants and all who fear him, whatever their social, political or other distinctions ("small and great" 11:18) to join in praising our God, using words drawn from the Old Testament (Ps 113:1; 115:13; 135:1).

A climax is reached in v 6 when John hears what resembles the voice of a vast multitude, a roaring waterfall or mighty thunderpeals (7:9; 14:2). This alleluia uses John's favourite term for God, the Almighty, and proclaims that God "has begun to reign" or "has taken sovereignty" (11:17). To explain this reign of God John uses three traditional ideas: the image of salvation as a wedding, Israel as Yahweh's bride, and the clean garments symbolising the Purity, loyalty, and faithfulness of the priestly people, the new Jerusalem (21:18ff). Joy is the dominant note symbolised by the readiness of the bride — the Church or the new Jerusalem. Some of these beautiful words were used by Handel in his famous "Hallelujah Chorus" and by Bach in his Cantata "Wachet Auf" ("Awake"). There is an obvious contrast between the gaudy prostitute and her merchant lovers and the Lamb and his chaste bride with her "fine linen bright and pure."

Jesus himself had used wedding and banquet imagery in his
kingdom parables (Mk 2:9; Jn 3:29; Mt 22:2ff; 25:1ff; Lk
14:15ff). The Old Testament had often used the marriage
symbol to describe the tender and intimate covenant union
between Yahweh and his people (Ezek 16:1ff; Hos 2:19; Is
54:5). John presupposes that his readers understand these
allusions. But he carefully explains that the fine linen symbolises the just and virtuous deeds of the saints (15:4). He also
noted that the "bride has prepared herself," probably meaning
obedient discipleship. Here we find another of those frequent
parallels to Matthew's gospel, his parable of the man without a
wedding garment. This wedding garment symbolised the new
life of the Christian, the fruitfulness and works of love which
it involved (Mt 22:11ff).

Typically John does not describe the actual wedding feast
of the Lamb — a mixing of metaphors to say the least. Rather
his aim is to give glimpses of future glory, to encourage his
community to be faithful to their commitment, to listen once
again and believe. John's lonely view from his island prison
illuminates the words attributed to the Irish poet and mystic
A. E. (George) Russell:

> I believe that the only news of any interest does not come from
> the great cities or from the councils of State, but from some
> lonely watcher on the hills who has a momentary glimpse of
> infinitude.

John's vision recalls the famous "I have a dream" speech of
Martin Luther King which so moved people in the turbulent
1960's. King was content with a glimpse of the promised land
as he said before his death in Memphis:

It really doesn't matter about me. I have been to the mountain top, and I have seen the promised land, and I know we shall go in.

After the marriage hymn an angel breaks in to command John to write down his fourth beatitude (1:3), thus stressing its importance. The words of the beatitude are very familiar because of their use in the Catholic Eucharistic Celebration just before communion: "Happy (Congratulations to) are those who are invited to the wedding feast of the Lamb." The angel solemnly stresses that these are true sayings from God and will repeat the same assurance about the whole book in the Epilogue (22:6). Some have wondered why such apparently simple words are singled out for emphasis. However, a closer reading shows that a beatitude, a summary of the whole gospel, is both a warning and a promise, a subtle contrast between the faithful and the unfaithful. Above all it is a reminder that our God is a calling God who does not force people but continually invites them to make decisions for their happiness. In 3:20 Jesus was pictured as standing at the door and knocking, while waiting for our invitation to the feast.

The angel's words are so impressive that John falls at his feet to worship him, a mistake which he repeats in 22:8f (Num 22:31; 1 Chr 21:16). Likewise, Cornelius the centurion was rebuked by Peter and the people at Lystra by Paul (Ac 10:25; 14:15). This reaction is unexpected because angels have frequently intervened in the text before this point. John seems to use the scene as a polemic against angel worship, which according to Colossians 2:8 was a temptation to some Christians. John insists on the traditional Jewish creed that there is only one God to be worshipped. Even angels are fellow servants and brothers whose task is to give witness to Jesus, for the witness of Jesus is the spirit of prophecy. This difficult sentence (v 10) seems to mean that all true prophecy testifies to Jesus as the faithful witness (1:5).

G. *The Coming of Christ and the Final Victory,* 19:11—20:5

Just when we think the book has come to an end we have another repetition of the basic cycle of themes: the suffering of the people of God as they struggle with the dreadful forces of evil, the seemingly inexplicable delay of justice, the assurance of ultimate vindication, and the punishment and triumph of God's Lamb. One can therefore appreciate the exclamation of one frustrated commentator: "Delay is the stuff of which Revelation is made." Perhaps at a more subtle level John is trying to cope with the problem of delay to restrain the yearnings of his community for instant justice while reassuring them that salvation is coming very soon. Like a symphony writer he takes up the now familiar images of the victorious Christ — the great dragon, the beast — and develops them in a new climactic synthesis to describe the final and irrevocable defeat of evil.

In the first scene (19:11-16) Christ is presented as the divine warrior like Yahweh in the Old Testament come to do battle with the enemies of his people (Ex 15:3; 2 Mac 3:22ff). However, John has transformed the traditional combat image because he does not actually describe any battle but only the victory and its results (v 20ff). The opening vision reminds us of the first vision (1:12ff) and, in a sense, is a climax of what has gone before. In 4:1 there was an open door to heaven while in 11:19 the temple in heaven was opened. Now heaven itself is thrown open (Ezek 1:1; Mk 1:10) and a series of what are sometimes called the seven last things unfold: the coming of Christ, the conquest of the dragon, the binding of Satan, the millennium, the defeat of the beast, the last judgment, and the new creation.

Although he does not explicitly say who the victorious rider on the white horse is, the parallels to the introductory vision (1:5, 14, 16; 3:7, 14) leave no doubt that Christ is involved. What he gives is a description of Christ in heaven and not precisely a return to earth, as some conclude. In fact the opening of the heavens suggests that what is happening is invisible to human eyes and therefore symbolic, rather than an exact description of what really is happening at the heart of the universe. Using some seven different terms, he describes the coming conqueror. These include four different names for the rider. Faithful and True (Hesed, Emeth) are the two key epithets of Yahweh throughout the Old Testament (1:7; 3:14). The meaning of the "name known to no one but himself" suggests that nobody has power or control over Yahweh to command him to do anything (2:17; 3:12). The third name "Word of God" is a a remarkable link with the prologue to John's gospel. It suggests that Jesus is God's way of speaking to us, his dynamic, creative, all powerful word in action (Is 55:11). This is the only text in the Bible where the full expression ("the Word of God"), which gave a title to a key document at Vatican II, is applied to Christ. The climax is the title "King of Kings and Lord of Lords," which was the title of the Lamb in 17:14. This title was written on the most

exposed part of his cloak which covered the thigh and proclaims the awesome and universal authority of Christ.

The symbol white stands for purity of life which is marked
by faithfulness and truth. The angelic troops are not in battle
dress but wear robes of fine linen, white and pure. The Victory
is achieved by judging with justice and not vindictiveness,
envy or lust for power which motivate other conquerors. The
continuing concern for justice in John, as well as in the rest of
the Bible, reveals the situation in which many of his audience
found themselves in the Roman Empire. Walter Brueggemann
characterises this aspect quite vividly (*The Land,* p 263):
"Apocalyptic is the visionary rage of those victimized by the
insanity of the present order."

The eyes "like a flame of fire" (1:14) enable this just ruler
to penetrate all deceptions. His many diadems contrast perhaps with the dragon's seven and the beast's ten (12:3; 13:1).
He has a name which only he himself knows yet that name is
Word of God and king over all other kings. He wears a cloak
that is dipped in blood. The blood is probably not that of his
enemies or the martyrs but, as is always mentioned with
Christ in the Apocalypse, his own (1:5; Is 63:1-3). This was
the conclusion of the early writers Hippolytus, Origen and
Andrew of Caesarea.

The strange symbol of the sharp sword protruding like a
tongue from his mouth was already given in 1:16; 2:12, 16
(Wis 18:14-16). The suggestion is that his only weapon, his
only power, is his word. Nevertheless, he is able to strike
down the nations (Is 11:3ff), to shepherd them with a rod of
iron (Ps 2:9), to tread out the winepress of God's wrath. These
three examples are Old Testament descriptions of the warrior-
Messiah (2:27: 14:17ff).

The second scene (v 17-21) is developed from Ezekiel 39:17ff where God commands birds of every kind to gather for a feast on the warriors and princes of God. John is obviously influenced by Ezekiel who describes his vision of the restored community with its new temple (Ezek 40:1ff). John's gruesome feast for the vultures which includes all the enemy "both small and great" is a grim contrast to the wedding feast of the Lamb. However, one should not exaggerate the hideousness of the scene as some commentators unfamiliar with the East seem to do. There, vultures and hyenas are a familiar feature. They perform a necessary and sanitary function in disposing of carcasses and returning them into the cycle of life. The scene is intended to warn the community of the consequences of the decisions they were making.

A careful reading of this section shows that John is not advocating violent means for his community (13:10). No real battle is fought. He only describes the mustering of the enemy, the capturing of the beast and the wonder-working false prophet (13:13; 16:13), and their casting alive into the fiery pool of burning sulphur. The victory is won by Christ's Word alone without any military help from the faithful. This view contrasts quite sharply with the other apocalypses of the period and, in particular, with the War Scroll of the Qumran sect. According to these documents the military help of the faithful is necessary in the final battle to defeat the impious. The Qumran scroll gave precise arrangements for the military formation at the vital battle.

John does not use the word hell or Gehenna as in the gospels but rather "fiery lake of burning sulphur" as if it were a familiar concept to his audience. According to Daniel 7:11 the beast was slain and its body thrown into the fire to be burned.

It was mentioned in 14:10 and will be the place for the devil (20:10), for Death and Hades (20:14), and for the wicked 21:8 (Mt 25:41). In the apocalyptic literature the "lake of torment" and the "furnace of the pit" contrast with the "place of rest" and the "paradise of joy" (2 Esd 7:36).

Having dealt with the immediate enemies of his community, the beasts, the kings of the earth and their followers, John now turns in a third scene (v 1-3) to the ultimate enemy who deceived the nations. He lists all his four names: the dragon, the ancient serpent, the devil or Satan (12:1ff). John sees an angel coming from heaven with the key of the abyss (9:1) and with a huge chain to lock up Satan for a thousand years (a millennium) so that he will not deceive the nations (2:20; 12:9). The abyss is shut and sealed over him. But his punishment differs from that of the others in that he will be given a short respite after the millennium. The meaning of this obviously symbolic story has puzzled commentators ever since. For Augustine, drawing on Jesus' reference to the binding of the strong man in Mark 3:27, the chaining meant that the devil was no longer permitted to tempt as much as he would. Since the time of Victorinus (died c. 303) some have interpreted it as the lives of believers, so that he no longer deceives them in contrast to the unbelievers. These explanations however do not fully explain the imprisoning of Satan in the Abyss or his release after the millennium. Perhaps there is a suggestion that evil can only be confined but not completely destroyed even by God. However, John has already insisted that the triumph of evil is very brief (12:14; 17:12). According to a Babylonian legend, in the beginning of time the god of light, Marduk, defeated and imprisoned in the depths of the sea, Tiamat the sea monster who stood for chaos. The myth went on to say that Tiamat would be released at the end of time when it would be defeated again by Marduk.

In the fourth scene (v 4-6) those who were beheaded for Christ are described as reigning with him for a thousand years while the other dead do not come to life until the millennium is over. The problems of the millennium, which we have already indicated in chapter one, are quite controversial. Only a cursory treatment can be attempted here. Three points should be kept in mind for any discussion of the issue. Firstly, this chapter is the only place in the Bible or in Jewish literature where we hear of a period of a thousand years (probably symbolic of a long period of God's time) when Satan is bound and Christ reigns with his martyrs. The second book of Enoch divides history into periods of a thousand years with the eighth as the eternal age. But it does not mention a Messiah. The fourth book of Ezra describes a messianic kingdom of 400 years. In 2 Baruch the Messiah will reign during the last, the most evil of four kingdoms, as long as the evil continues. Secondly, the notion is only of lesser importance in the two paragraphs in which it is introduced. These paragraphs deal primarily with the binding of Satan and the first joyful resurrection of the martyrs. Thirdly, many orthodox Jews today believe that when the Messiah comes he will reign on earth for a limited period.

John begins with a vision of thrones (v 4) and notes that those sitting on them were empowered to give judgement. He also sees the spirits of those who were publicly executed, literally "killed with an axe." These are probably the 144,000 "first fruits" described in 14:1-5. They are the happy (1:3) and holy ones who (now) share in the first resurrection and who came to life again and reigned with Christ as priests for a thousand years. Since Augustine, most commentators have understood the words to mean baptism, the spiritual resurrection or new birth. Some interpret it as the triumph of the Church. The second resurrection would then refer to the resurrection of the just and the unjust at the final general resurrection (*City of God*, 20:9f). The second death, (2:11) according to a Targum on Dt. 33:6, meant exclusion from resurrection to the world to come. However, neither Augustine's interpretation nor that of any other commentator is able to account for every detail in John's description.

John's fifth scene (v 7-10) describes the releasing of Satan from prison once the millennium is over. John unfortunately does not explain why or how evil people have survived the previous destruction. He seems to be using the story to suggest that while the definitive defeat of Satan took place at the crucifixion of Jesus, a further assault of evil on the beloved city is to be expected. The scene is another example of John's surprising delay of the final, total victory. His treatment of Satan suggests the constant resilience of the forces of evil in the world. Is he warning his community not to take the struggle with evil too lightly? Defeated in heaven by Michael, Satan continued to reign on earth (12:7-9). Again Satan was defeated and locked up for a limited time by an angel in 20:1ff. Now he is loose for a third and final war of deception to be conquered by God himself. Deceived by Satan, the nations in all four corners of the earth muster for war the troops of Gog and Magog. Numerous as the sands of the sea (Gn 22:17), they surround God's people and the beloved city (16:16). Our writer seems to have turned Ezekiel's Gog from the mythical land of Magog into two people Gog and Magog (Ezek 38:2). Three times Ezekiel predicted that God would attack Israel living in security. God's people are rescued by fire from heaven which consumes their enemies. John's picture of destruction is much less detailed than Ezekiel's. In Ezekiel God shows his greatness and holiness and makes himself known to the many nations by summoning every terror, pestilence and bloodshed, flooding rain and hailstones, fire and brimstone.

In Jewish tradition the "city he loves" would refer to a restored and renewed Jerusalem (Hab 12:22; Ps 87:2). However, drawing on John's previous references in 3:12 and 11:2ff, the wider symbolism of the faithful Christian community seems to be the meaning here. John has polarized the world into two cities, the city of Satan, his beasts and the harlot, and the city of God where his Lamb reigns.

John's message here is that the final judgement of evil is swift and total. Satan is cast into the lake of fire with his evil minions to be tortured forever (14:10). Again he points out that it is achieved by God and not by human armies (19:19). Even the Messiah is not mentioned here as conquering Gog and Magog.

John still has more to say even after the conquest of Satan. In his sixth scene of only five verses (vv 11-15) he gives an account, impressive in its stark simplicity, of the last judgement and the destruction of the ultimate enemy, Death and Hades. Influenced by Daniel 7:9-14, the majestic scene opens with the vision of a great white throne and "him who sat upon it," a phrase which probably means God the Father. If so, John differs from the normal New Testament teaching which assigns the final judgement to the Son (Mt 7:22f; 25:31ff; Jn 5:22; Ac 17:31; 2 Cor 5:10). The awesome presence of God is marvellously portrayed in the statement that "the earth and sky fled from his presence until there was found no place for them." The scene is also set for the new heavens and the new earth to replace those which were destroyed (21:1ff). John sees all the dead, "the great and the lowly," standing before the throne (20:4; 6:17). Even the sea, the place of the unburied, a concept abhorrent to many in the ancient world, gives up its dead to resurrection.Death and Hades also gave up their dead. This scene has been unforgettably immortalised by what has been described as the greatest work of the world's greatest artist, Michelangelo in his fresco of the Last Judgement. His "three thousand square feet of impending apocalypse" dominates the altar in the Sistine Chapel in Rome. The idea is strikingly expressed in the Sequence *Dies Irae* of the Requiem Mass and has been set to music by many famous composers.

"And books were opened, and another book was opened, the book of life." (20:12; cf. 3:5). In the former were contained the records of each person's deeds and in the latter the register of their names. John agrees with the common New Testament teaching about God's ultimate justice that all are judged according to their recorded deeds (2:23; 7:14). We are justified by faith but judged by deeds or works of faith. He is pointing out that the deeds of each person, whether Christian or not, have ultimate significance. Finally, Paul's cry about the last enemy, death, is fulfilled (1 Cor 15:26; Is 25:8). Death and its abode Hades, like the dragon and the beasts, are cast into the lake of fire. John ends with a warning to his community: "and if anyone's name was not found written in the book of life, he was thrown into the lake of fire."

H. The New Creation, 21:1–22:5

After a long and somewhat wearing journey, which symbolises the pilgrimage of life with its repeated cycles of frustrating
struggles, failures and partial victories, John finally explodes
with his wonderful vision of the New Creation, a vision that
has inspired countless poets, musicians, artists, and above all,
ordinary Christians ever since. J. B. Moffatt in the *Expositor's
Greek New Testament*, has strikingly caught the freshness of
John's hauntingly beautiful finale to his symphonic work.

> From the smoke and pain and heat of the preceding scenes it is
> a relief to pass into the clear, clean atmosphere of the eternal
> morning where the breath of heaven is sweet and the vast city
> of God sparkles like a diamond in the radiance of his presence.

John has disposed of the dragon, the beasts, the judgement,
and the ultimate enemy, death. Now he moves on to give a
positive, joyful, and truly magnificent description of the New
Creation, of the risen life with God.

First he provides an introductory paragraph in which his
basic themes are enunciated. These themes are the new
creation (v 1), the fulfillment of the Exodus covenant presence
(v 3), the new city (v 2f), the eternal happiness of God's
people (v 4). These themes are further elaborated in the
remaining sections, the new creation (vv 5-8), the new Jerusalem (vv 9-21), God's presence (vv 22-27), paradise regained
(22:1-5). In brief, paradise lost has been regained. Therefore
this whole section is a fitting conclusion to the whole biblical
story. It contains many direct allusions to the opening three
chapters of Genesis: God's presence with his people as inti-

mate as in Eden, the ending of suffering and death, the removal of the curse, the restoration of the tree of life. It also describes the fulfillment of the promises to the victors of the seven churches (ch 2-3).

INTRODUCTION, 21:1–4

The basic theme of the vision is the new heaven and earth, a semitic way of describing the whole of creation. According to Genesis all of the good God's creation is good. There is no basis for the kind of dualism which sees matter or any part of creation as intrinsically evil. Yet there is a spiritual dualism between the kingdom of God and the kingdom of the dragon and his allies. Human sin has corrupted the earth with consequences in all our relationships to God, fellow human beings, self, the material world. Fear, greed, and exploitation are prominent. Isaiah summed up the cure for what was wrong with the world under the single word "justice." He hoped for a new exodus and a new creation of heaven and earth (Is 65:7). According to Matthew 19:28, Jesus spoke of all being made new in the kingdom of the Son of Man. Similar expectations are found in Paul (Gal 6:15; 2 Cor 5:17) and Peter (2 Pt 3:10).

The word used for new by John does not mean another model like the old, a recent model of the old one. Rather, the meaning is new in kind, fresh in quality. What makes it new is especially the centrality of the Lamb and the special presence of God. We commonly think of the afterlife as life in heaven. But here it seems to be heaven on earth symbolised by a holy city, the new Jerusalem. John describes this new creation from both a negative and a positive point of view. On the one hand

John excludes from his new creation at least seven evils including the hostile sea (21:1), death, mourning, crying, pain (v 4), whatever deserves a curse (22:3), night (22:5). The sea in particular symbolised chaos (13:1). On the other hand the new creation is symbolised by a new city of Jerusalem. Three times the city is described as a city "descending from heaven" (3:12, 12:2, 10), in other words, a different kind of city, a divine creation. The old Jerusalem was also described as holy and a bride (Is 52:1; 61:10). But it was unfaithful and guilty of the blood not only of the prophets and apostles but also of the Lord himself (11:8). Babylon was its synonym. The new city is beautifully described as "one like a bride adorned for her husband," the Lamb (21:9; 19:7). A great heavenly voice interprets the scene. Three times it says that God is with them. He is their God. The same Greek word used for God's tabernacling ("pitching his tent") among his people is found in John 1;14: "The word became flesh and tabernacled among us." The hopes of the Old Testament are fulfilled (Ex 25:8; Ezek 37:36f; Lev 26:11ff). The valley of tears will be no more because of God's tender motherly love (7:15). The story of the Bible is the search by God in history to restore the communion with his people that was lost when Adam and Eve hid from their God (Gn 3:8). Dietrich Bonhoeffer's remarks on this passage in Genesis in his *Creation and Fall* are to the point:

> 'Adam, where are you?' With this word the Creator calls Adam forth out of his conscience. Adam must stand before his Creator ... Come out of your hiding place, from your self-reproach, your covering, your secrecy, your self-torment, from your vain remorse. Confess to yourself, do not lose yourself in religious despair, be yourself, Adam ... Where are you? Stand before your Creator!

ALL THINGS NEW, 21:5–8

Now, for only the second time in the book, God himself speaks. The command to write and the divine title Alpha and Omega also take the reader back to the opening chapter (1:11, 19) and provide a kind of inclusive bridge for the whole book and its interpretation. God insists that his words "see I make all things new" are trustworthy and true (3:14; 19:9). With the same verb which he used to show that the judgement of the world was complete, the all powerful God says of his new creation: "It is done" (16:17). This is like the phrase "and so it happened" after each of God's creative words in the first chapter of Genesis. Here is the key message of hope to be communicated to the churches. Lest there be any doubters, God himself authenticates the fact that he the Omega has already completed his new creation. But before John describes the holy city he insists that there is a fundamental option or choice to be made. To anyone who thirsts (recognises his need) God will grant "to drink without cost from the spring of life-giving water" (7:17; Jn 4:14; Mt 5:6; Rom 3:24). One has only to come and drink. In lands where water was such an essential commodity, salvation is beautifully described by the symbolism of a fountain and a river (22:1) The phrase "the one who conquers" takes us back to the promises to the seven churches. Their inheritance will be the personal promise of intimate sonship made to King David (2 Sm 7:14; Gal 4:7; Rom 8:17).

Recalling the criticisms of the churches in the seven letters, John gives a blunt warning by cataloging those heading for the lake of fire (19:20). The cowardly head the list. It is not fear as such that is condemned but lack of endurance. True faith refuses to compromise in the storms of life (Mk

4:40; Mt 8:26). These are linked to those who are unbeliev-
ing especially in a time or situation which calls for witness,
and the polluted, a word used of those who take part in the
impurities of idolatry (17:4; Rom 2:22). The description
"murderers" alludes especially to the killing of the faithful
(17:6). Fornicator is a derogatory term for those who take
part in pagan rites such as emperor worship. Ephesus was
full of sorcerers (Ac 19:19). They tried to deceive people into
false religion (9:21; 22:15). Idolaters are those who worship
false gods, whose home is Babylon and not the holy city.
Liars and all kinds of untruth have regularly been condemned by John (2:2; 3:9; 14:5; 21:8).

For John, plague and blessing are two sides of the one coin
throughout his book. According to Paul S. Minear (*New
Testament Apocalyptic*, p 135f), it is sentimentality which
encourages readers to ignore such hard sayings and even
quietly to exclude them from their lectionaries. This distaste
for John's realism turns a beautiful poem into an "ego trip"
for pious souls and makes belief in a future life a barrier to
honest religion. It promotes self-interest and greed which a
truly religious faith ought to destroy.

THE NEW JERUSALEM, 21:9–21

Finally after his long mental journey, John, with a series of
joyful and striking images describes the new Jerusalem, the
bride of the Lamb. Beginning with a description of the gates
and the walls (vv 9-14), he then describes an angel measuring the city (vv 15-17) and finally the precious stones which
are the building materials of the city (vv 19-21).

John's introduction (an angel of the seven bowls saying, "Come, and I will show you...") makes a deliberate parallel between his description in 17:1 of the great prostitute and the Lamb's bride, the holy city. To see the prostitute for what she was, John needed to go into the desert. To see the holy city, he is carried in the spirit (1:10) to a great and lofty mountain, the symbol of the presence of God and his heavenly throne (1:10). In this he resembles Ezekiel whose vision of the New Jerusalem he will reinterpret (Ezek 40:2ff). Ezekiel had described a city whose name was "The Lord is there," a city with four high walls, and three gates on each side named for the twelve tribes (Ezek 48:30-35). Like Moses, John stands on Mt. Pisgah to survey the promised land for the faithful.

There is no basis here for what is called "celestial geographising," as if the city descended like a huge space satellite on earth. The city, John insists, is God's new creation and is the antithesis of the city of Babel or any product of human activity, evolution, or development.

The new city (v 11) "shone with the glory of God." To elaborate on this ethereal beauty and unsurpassed loveliness John uses the images of priceless jewels, brilliant colours, and shining lights. What impresses him about the gates are the angel guards or protectors and the names on the gates (the twelve tribes) and the foundations (the twelve apostles). The old walls of Jerusalem have been recently excavated and its triple gates and huge foundation stones measuring 5' x 4' x 30' and weighing nearly 100 tons, have been laid bare. But what is significant is the continuity between the twelve tribes of the Old Testament and the apostles of the New Testament (Mt 19:28; Lk 22:30).

The heavenly city is so large that only an angel with a golden rod can measure it (11:1). This measuring reveals the perfection, size, and quality of God's city. It is a perfect cube of about 1,400 miles in length, breadth and height.These are clearly symbolic numbers representing the infinity of God. The cube shape reminds one of the cube-shaped Holy of Holies in the temple which the city replaced (1 K 6:20). In vv 18-21 John describes in detail the building materials — no ordinary stone but precious and semi-precious stones (Is 54:11f). The symbolism is not one of riches and luxury but rather an extension of the holinesss and glory of God. The jasper and crystal of his throne room are found here (4:3, 6). The foundation stones are adorned with twelve precious stones. These recall the high priest's breastplate (Ex 28:17-20), the jewels on the garments of the King of Tyre, (Ezek 28:13) and also the signs of the zodiac. According to Josephus (Antiq 3:186) and Philo, each tribal standard in Israel carried a sign of the zodiac. For Judah the tribe of Christ (7:5), the sign was Aries, the ram with the amethyst stone. But the order of the zodiac is reversed, perhaps implying some disapproval and suggesting that God's order is different. The description of the twelve gates, each made from a single pearl, gives us our phrase "the pearly gates of heaven." The city itself and its streets were of pure gold like clear glass, symbolizing purity and perfection.

GOD'S PRESENCE, 21:22-27

John suddenly switches to describe the life within this incredible city, a life characterised by light, quality of life, health, and eternity. Every ancient city was marked by its temple. Ezekiel had spent four long chapters describing the new temple in detail (40-43). John simply says "I saw no temple in the city" because the Lord and the Lamb are the temple. He has already depicted the whole city as a cube like the Holy of Holies. There is no need for such religious institutions because their hopes and purpose are fulfilled. In this the Apocalypse differs from the normal Jewish vision and speculations about the rebuilt temple in the world to come (3:12; 7:15).

Secondly, as Isaiah had foretold, there is no need for sun or moon because there will be no night (Is 60:19-20). God's glory is a sufficient light or lamp. The word glory in the bible often suggests the visible manifestation and reflection of God's awesome presence. The word light has a different connotation for an Eastern person than for one from the West for whom it has more intellectual stress, illustrating the difference between knowledge and ignorance. In the East it expressed living rather than thinking, the difference between security and danger. For night was the time of fear and darkness, of danger from wild beasts and thieves (Ps 27:1; Is 9:2; 60:1, 19). This emphasis on light at the end has given rise to the frequent description of the Apocalypse as a tunnel book with light in the opening chapters and at the end and in between a long stretch of darkness, doom, plagues, and vivid monsters which thunder past, bewildering and stunning the onlookers. "Let there be light" was the first word God spoke in the Bible. Now it is fully realized (2 Cor 4:6).

Thirdly, there is no division between the city and the gentiles and the kings of the earth. The fact that these were destroyed in 13:7ff and 19:1 and healed in 22:2 shows the author's lack of concern for agreement in details. His point is that the ancient hope that Israel would be a light to the nations will be fulfilled. The kings of the earth, the symbols of political power structures, are important in the Apocalypse. Here they bring their wealth and splendour into God's city. Thus Christ will really be the King of Kings (17:14).

Fourthly, heaven's doors remain open always (3:8, 20; Is 60:11). Even the gentiles will have free access. No fear for security by night will demand closed gates (Jn 20:19). Yet no kind of impurity, idolatry or falsehood will be in this city (21:8; 17:4f). Only those redeemed to life by the Lamb will be found there (3:5). Thus John exhorts his readers once again to repentance and to full commitment to the Lamb.

PARADISE REGAINED, 22:1-5

Coming to the end of his vision, John reaches back to the opening chapters of Genesis and to Ezekiel 40:1ff for his images of paradise restored. The semi-desert character of most of the biblical world made water and trees into powerful symbols of paradise or eternal life. All through the Bible water symbolised the cleansing and salvific life-giving activity of God (7:17; 8:10; Is 44:3; Jn 3:5; 4:14). The river of the water of life recalls the river which flowed through the garden in Eden (Gn 2:10). Psalm 46:4 described a river whose streams gladden the city of God. Ezekiel 47:1ff described a continually growing river flowing out from the temple until it brought life and fish to the Dead Sea. John's river clear as crystal flows not from a mere temple but from the throne of God and the Lamb and up and down the middle of the streets in the city.

Ezekiel's river had many trees beside it bearing fruit monthly. Their leaves were for healing (Ezek 47:7, 12). John had promised the faithful Ephesians that they would "eat of

the tree of life which is in the paradise of God" (2:7; Gn 2:17).
John now speaks of trees of life with abundant fruit twelve
times a year and leaves which bring healing to the nations
(21:24; 7:9; 19:21; Joel 1:14; 2:15). His description symbolises
the widespread healing effects of the death of the Lamb.

The remark about the absence of anything deserving a
curse recalls Zechariah's prophecy (4:11) that Jerusalem
would dwell in security because God's ban or anathema on
the city was removed. Perhaps there is a suggestion that the
curse pronounced in Genesis 3:17f is removed. Curses and the
punishments involved were important in the Old Testament
(Dt 28:1ff). Instead of any accursed thing (a word found only
here in the Greek Bible), the throne of God and the Lamb will
be there. There are no restrictions on entry into God's
presence such as Moses and the high priests suffered (Heb 9:7;
Ex 33:20ff). Heaven consists in his servants worshipping him,
seeing him face to face, bearing his name on their foreheads
(Ex 28:36-38), living in his light, and reigning forever. It is a
paradoxical combination of serving and reigning. For nowhere
are subjects or underlings mentioned.

I. Epilogue, 22:6–21

A spontaneous reaction to John's vision is that it seems to be
an incredible story. In his concluding verses John tries to leave
his audience with a strong sense of both the authenticity and
the urgency of what he has been saying. At first sight this
conclusion looks like quite a disorderly staccato jumble. But a
more careful reading shows the work of an artist who cleverly
sounds again the voices of his introduction (1:1-8) and lets us

hear in succession the voices of the revealing angel, Jesus himself, the Spirit, the bride or the Church, and finally the prophet John himself. The first two verses (v 6f) summarise the three basic themes of the conclusion. First the revealing angel authenticates the book as containing words "trustworthy and true" (3:14). These words are probably polemical against the prophetic claims of the Nicolaitans and other apocalyptic speculators. The repeated warning against angel worship (19:10) and the simple command "Worship God," i.e. alone, are significant. John claims for his work a fourfold authentication: God himself (1:1; 22:6, 16); Christ (1:1; 22:16, 18); the angels who mediated it (1:1; 22:16); John, who identifies himself only in 1:1, 4, 9 now names himself and authenticates his writing as a prophetic writing to be read as a source of encouragement and warning in the Churches (22:7ff).

The command not to seal his book because the time is near is in sharp contrast to the command given to Daniel (Dn 8:26; 12:4ff). Daniel is a literary fiction claiming to be written in the sixth century B.C. about events in the second century. Actually it is also a book written about contemporary events. John's command "seal not" is an invitation to publish the message, because no secret wisdom is involved. John solemnly concludes his book with a blessing and a curse in true biblical style, which warns against any tampering with the contents or message of the book (Dt 4:1ff; 1 Cor 16:22).

Secondly, the conclusion stresses four times (vv 6, 7, 12, 20) a theme found only three times in the rest of the book (1:1; 2:16; 3:11), that Christ will come soon and that the interval before his return will be short.

Thirdly, the note of warning and blessing shows that John's

work is a pastoral work not mainly concerned with historical information or predictions about the future. The final two of his seven beatitudes (1:7) are found here. The sixth beatitude, which is a summary of the first one (v 7; 1:3), pronounces blessing on those who obey or put into practice his prophetic warning to worship one God and to be ready to endure the consequences. The last beatitude (v 14) parallels 7:14. It blesses those who wash (present tense) their robes in the Lamb's blood and thus identify with Jesus' death. They have free access to the tree of life (22:2) and enter the city through its gates (21:25). The latter are in contrast to the seven categories of those outside (Mt 8:12). These were already listed in 22:15 except for "the dogs," a rather derogatory term for evil people, often Gentiles in the Bible (Ps 22:16; Phil 3:2; Dt 23:18; Mt 15:26). When Jesus returns he will reward each according to his or her conduct (20:13). Verse 11 "Let the wicked continue in their wicked ways" appears at first sight fatalistic. But John's basic aim is to invite his community to repentance. The Spirit and the Bride, the Church, invite the thirsty, those in need, to take the water of life without price.

The whole book closes on a note of longing or hope and a greeting of grace. The last verses are not unlike 1 Cor 16:22-24 with its "if anyone" formula curse, "*Maranatha*" invitation and concluding benediction grace. John's aim is that Jesus' grace will be with his community (1:4) so that they will enthusiastically respond to Jesus' testimony that he is coming soon: "Amen. Come, Lord Jesus."

5

THE INTERPRETATION OF THE APOCALYPSE IN HISTORY

Among biblical scholars in every age there has always been a keen interest in the Apocalypse. Of all the books in the Bible it ranks among those which have received the most commentaries and studies. An examination of the second century Christian writings, for example, shows that the Apocalypse is the New Testament book most quoted. The following overview of the different approaches to the Apocalypse down through the centuries is intended to provide a deeper base for the spirituality of the reader. The intention is also to show that there is an arbitrary quality about every age's exegesis. This systematic survey of the struggles of the community of scholars is an indication of the nature of the evidence available. It warns about the impossibility of total objectivity and neutrality and shows that final and fully satisfactory answers are often not achievable. Further, a survey helps to avoid superficiality in interpretation, to enrich and widen one's horizon leading to unsuspected depths of the profound, many-sided work which is the Apocalypse. A summary however does not do adequate justice to the detail of each position. Its purpose is to highlight how these approaches differ rather than show what they have in common.

1. The Millenarianist Interpretation

This, the oldest interpretation, is based on a rather literal interpretation of Apoc 20:1-6, a Christian adaptation of Jewish speculations found especially in Daniel, 2 Esdras, and Enoch. This passage speaks of the incarceration of Satan and a thousand year reign of the faithful on earth with Christ before the final victory. Millenarianism or Chiliasm (from the Greek word for 1,000) was frequently taught and accepted within the Christian Church particularly during the first hundred years and by such orthodox writers as Papias, Justin Martyr, Irenaeus, Hippolytus of Rome, the historian Eusebius and the writer of the Epistle of Barnabas. In those years the Church was wrestling with the problem of the realization of Jesus' promise of the coming kingdom, for, despite his promises, life continued after his death in much the same fashion as before. The Roman Empire was at best neutral and often quite hostile to the early Christians. But when large numbers in the Roman Empire were converted, including the Emperor Constantine, the antagonism towards the Empire gradually weakened.

Further, the association of millenarianism with the second century Montanists who went off into the Phrygian wilderness, expecting to see the heavenly Jerusalem descend from heaven, brought this interpretation into disrepute. The growing influence of Greek thought upon Christian theology helped to discredit it for centuries as well. It received a fatal blow from the third century Alexandrian Christian theologian, Origen. He, with his allegorical approach, was interested more in the spiritual and the metaphysical rather than the historical elements. He placed the focus of the kingdom's manifestation not upon the world but within the soul of the believer. When Christianity triumphed over the Roman Empire it was Augustine (354-430) with his allegorical and spiritual interpretation who provided the definitive interpretation that dominated Western civilization until the intellectual revolution of the seventeenth century. This explanation was accepted by the leading reformers and has been accepted by many Christians to this day.

For Augustine, the millennium was the spiritual condition into which the Church as a body had entered with the coming of the Holy Spirit at Pentecost. The Church represented the City of God in contrast to the City of the World ruled by Satan. The thrones of Apoc 20:4 are those of the Catholic hierarchy which has the power of binding and loosing. No imminent divine intervention in history or decisive battle was to be expected. The final spiritual battle had already been fought. Although Satan was reduced to lordship in this world, eventually his small patrimony would be taken from him and God would fully triumph. With the dominance of the Augustinian view, apocalypticism went underground and was voiced chiefly by dissidents and rebels. After the Reformation, the Anabaptists, the Bohemian and Moravian Brethren, the seventeenth century Independents in England, and the Pietist Movement in the seventeenth and eighteenth centuries had millenarian views. The great upheaval of the French Revolution and the industrialisation of the West caused a new wave of millenarian sects including the Irvingites, the Seventh-day Adventists, Jehovah's Witnesses, the Latter-day Saints (Mormons), and others who are often described as Fundamentalists. In the United States the rise of such groups increased during such times of national crises as the 1930's, the 1970's, and the world wars in the twentieth century. After World War I the theme of the golden age of the millennium assumed an increasingly central role among many Pentecostal and Holiness groups and in particular among the most conservative Protestants, the Fundamentalists. The latter received their name from their rigid emphasis on such fundamentals as the virgin birth, inerrancy of Scripture, and the literal return of Christ on clouds of glory.

However, Millenarianism has never been formally rejected by orthodox Christianity, apart from occasional criticism such as the view at the council of Ephesus (431) that it was a deviation and a fable, and the reply from the Holy Office of the Vatican on 21 July 1944 that it was not "safe" teaching. The prevalent view among biblical scholars is that there is no sufficient justification for the theory in either scripture or tradition. Many scholars accept the view of the French scholar, Boismard, that the thousand years corresponds to the earthly period of the Church from the early persecutions to the end of the world. Thus the symbolic description of the return of Christ in 19:1ff is probably best understood as another account or doublet of the version given later in 20:7-11.

2. Recapitulation

A constant temptation, when reading ancient books, is to presume that they are written by authors with a modern, orderly plan, historical or otherwise, with one part following logically from the other. A careful reading of the Apocalypse shows that it constantly repeats the same events under different forms. Not unlike the Book of Daniel, the author tends to overlap and to provide alternate accounts of the same events. This theory of Recapitulation, which admirably simplifies the interpretation, goes back to Victorinus of Pettau (Austria) who was martyred under Diocletian in 303. The millenarianist Victorinus, who has given us the oldest extant commentary on the Apocalypse (*Patrologia Latina* 5, 281-334), concluded that there is a chronological progression as far as the sixth seal. After that, there is an account of the final persecution in the "seven trumpets" section (8:2-11:19), a description which is then repeated in a more complete form in the remaining "seven bowls" section. This approach was developed with greater precision by the Donatist Tyconius (c. 390) and adopted by the influential Augustine and thereafter by many commentators both ancient and modern. The French scholar E. B. Allo (1921) has provided a detailed exposition in his commentary. Following on the septet of letters (ch 2-3), which are not strictly prophetic, but which deal with the current state of the churches in Asia, the two septets of seals and trumpets describe the future of the world from a profane point of view. Chapters 12 — 21:8 cover the same period of the history of humanity, from Jesus' exaltation to his parousia, emphasizing the role of the Church. Thus, the last plagues (15:1) do not follow chronologically the septet of trumpets.

Likewise, the millennium does not describe a special period of history but rather the same period from a different point of view. It describes the earthly phase of the Kingdom of God established with the Resurrection. However, this sweeping parallel interpretation does not satisfy all scholars such as R. H. Charles and E. Lohmeyer, some of whom believe that John has some succession of events in mind. Their conclusion is based on such verses as 15:1 —

> seven angels with seven plagues, which are the last,
> for with them the wrath of God is ended.

One can therefore conclude that there is a steady linear progress through the book to a climax but not in the way that successive events are forecast. Rather, different aspects of the same subject are revealed in a variety of images so that the basic realities are continually illuminated. Not surprisingly a comparison with the development of a symphony or chorale has often been suggested.

3. *World History*

In the twelfth century a number of writers began to move away from the traditional, individualistic, and spiritual exegesis of the Apocalypse. This new approach, formulated into a coherent theory of hermeneutics by Joachim of Fiore (c. 1132-1202), considered the Apocalypse to be a detailed prophecy and forecast of identifiable historical events. Joachim divided the history of the world into three great periods. The first was the age of the Father, the Old Testament, in which people lived under the Law for forty-two generations. The second was the age of the Son, the New Testament, in which people lived under grace for forty-two generations of thirty years each, up to the year 1260. The third, the age of the Spirit would be inaugurated about 1260. New religious orders would defend the Church against its enemies and succeed in converting the whole world to the contemplative life. These optimistic expectations had a widespread influence on many people during the later Middle Ages, especially the Spiritual Franciscans and Fraticelli who drew revolutionary conclusions from Joachim's predictions. But Joachim also saw in the septenaries of the Apocalypse seven periods in the history of the Church. His theory was further refined by Nicholas of Lyra who wrote the first biblical commentary to be printed, a work which became very popular. The first period (ch 2-3), was the struggle between the Apostles and the Jews (2nd-3rd century); the second (ch 4-7), the Martyrs, against the Romans such as Diocletian (4th-7th century); the third (ch 8-11), the Doctors, against the Arians (8th-11th century); the fourth (ch 12-14), the Virgins, the Religious Orders against the Muslims (12th-14th century); the fifth (ch 15-18), the Church against Babylon, the degenerate holy Empire. This was the period of Joachim himself in which he found some extraordinary coincidences with the Apocalypse. He believed that the fall of Jerusalem in 1187 and Saladin's triumph over the Christians in the East, was a sign that the Church's suffering was reaching its climax. The sixth period would be the age of Antichrist (ch 19) and the seventh, the Millennium leading to the final consummation (ch 20-22).

Continuing the line of Joachim, John Wycliffe (c. 1329-84) in his *Dialogus* believed that the Pope was the Antichrist. Luther interpreted the Two Beasts as the Pope and the

Emperor. Other candidates have included Luther himself, Napoleon, Hitler, and Stalin. The Adventists announced the end of this evil world for 1843, then 22 October 1844, while the Jehovah Witnesses chose 1914. These interpretations are generally based on a misunderstanding of the literary form of apocalypse and its confusion with a rather limited understanding of prophecy as if its main emphasis was to predict the historical future in detail. The constant problem has been to revise one's predictions whenever the events turn out otherwise. Today serious exegetes do not search for detailed applications of the Apocalypse.

4. Eschatological

The arbitrariness of the world history interpretations led to a salutary reaction in the sixteenth and seventeenth centuries especially among Catholic exegetes such as the Spanish Jesuit F. Ribeira in his 1591 commentary. His interpretation was continued in the twentieth century by Lohmeyer (1926), Baldensperger (1928), Wilkenhauser (1947), Camps (1958), and Lilye (1959). Essentially, this approach suggests that John is only speaking of the parousia, an event which he considered to be very near. Ribeira's commentary is often described as one of the first commentaries on the Apocalypse in which a scientific interpretation is accepted. For Ribeira, only the first five seals treat the history of the primitive Church, from the preaching of the Apocalypse up to Trajan's reign. From the sixth seal to the end, everything refers to the end-time (eschatology). Therefore the book is basically composed of two parts. Up to chapter 11 we find a description of the calamities before the reign of the Antichrist. From chapters

12-20 the author predicts the reign of the Antichrist and the accompanying persecution.

The key idea is probably valid. In contrast to a historian who studies the present in the light of the past, a prophetic writer explains the present in the light of the future. John interprets the present not only in the light of a past event, the resurrection of Jesus, but also in the light of his definitive coming. However, not only has his future coming an important influence on the present but Jesus is the Lord of all history, especially the present critical situation. He exercises a hidden, though real, control over the present and over the forces of evil which are hostile to his people.

5. Historicising

A reaction to the eschatological approach was led by the Louvain Professor, Henten (1547). He believed that at least part of the book referred to contemporary events such as first century emperors, revolts and invasions. He was the first to conclude that the prophetic part of the Apocalypse should be divided into two sections. The first (ch 6-11) referred to the abrogation of Judaism and the second (ch 12-19) to the destruction of Roman paganism. He also saw the Apocalypse as announcing the persecution of the Church by Islam and the destruction of Islam. The Spanish Jesuit, Alcazar, further developed Henten's twofold division to produce the first adequately scientific exegesis of the Apocalypse (1614). For Alcazar the first seal refers to the apostolic proclamation and the triumph of the Gospel, while the sixth refers to the siege of Jerusalem. Chapter 7 describes the salvation of the Christians in Palestine. Chapters 8-9 deal with the Jewish sufferings during the Roman invasion. At chapter 10 the Gospel passes from the Jews to the Gentiles. Chapter 11 treats of the destruction of Jerusalem — the two witnesses symbolize the renewed Church and a part of the Jews who are converted. With chapter 12 the second part of the book begins. The woman is the Jewish-Christian community which brings forth at Rome the Gentile-Christian Church and is persecuted by Nero. The first Beast in chapter 13 is the Roman Empire. The second Beast is the wisdom of the flesh and the number 666. The seven cups signify the progressive victory of Christianity over the Roman Empire. In chapter 19:1ff one arrives at the complete conversion of the Roman Empire. Constantine is the angel who imprisons Satan to begin the millennium which is destined to last until the end of the world. Note the absence of the theory of recapitulation in Alcazar's rather vague prophecy and of any detailed programme for the future of the Church.

Other enthusiasts for the historicizing interpretation such as Bossuet, Cerfaux, and Gelin, differ on the amount of contemporary or past material to be found in the Apocalypse. In 1644 the Protestant interpreter Grotius repudiated the antipapal interpretation. However, he found the revolt of Bar Cochba in chapter 11, Simon the Magician in chapter 12, and Apollonius of Tyana in chapter 13. Grotius' approach was also developed by the German "Zeitgeschichtlich" school, which adopted a rationalistic approach, excluding the prophetic and supernatural. The Apocalypse was little more than a symbolic history of the contemporary events of the writer with a merely imaginative portrayal of the end of the world. Typical of this approach was Ernst Renan (Paris, 1871). He saw correspondence to the terrible events of the Jewish war of 67-69 in the famine prices of 6:6-7; a volcanic eruption of the island of Thera (near Patmos) in 8:8; a meteor causing water infection in 8:10; an eclipse or the terrible storm of 10 January in 8:11; the sulphurous emissions of Pozzuoli (ancient Puteoli, near Naples) in the smoky shaft of 9:2; and two important persons of the Jerusalem Church in the two witnesses in chapter 11. The influential interpretation of E. F. Scott in 1949 sees the Apocalypse as an occasional writing referring to the events of the first century Church just like the other New Testament epistles. Its intended audience was not future generations of Christians but the faithful of a determined period of time. This epistle was at the same time a prophetic writing which gives to Christians of all times the certitude of the triumph of God's kingdom. For Scott the Apocalypse therefore is no longer the mysterious book which it was to our ancestors. The difficulties that remain are puzzles like those we find in the Gospels and in Paul. Because its general meaning lies on the surface, the Apocalypse according to Scott has become in some ways the simplest and most intelligible book in the New Testament.

The nineteenth century saw the gradual triumph of the historical-critical approach over all other approaches to interpretation. This approach was based on the theory that a work must be interpreted in terms of the contemporary background of the person who wrote the book. The theory was fine but the problem which gradually emerged was that the real historical horizon of the author is to a large extent lost and his historical allusions are often quite vague to us. We have access only to a minute proportion, and not necessarily the most useful proportion, of the information available to the earliest reader. Some sixty years passed before we find any references to the book and over a hundred before any writer examines it at length.

6. The Comparative Method

Towards the end of the nineteenth century, under the influence of such scholars as Gunkel and Bousset a search was carried out for the origin of the different images in the Apocalypse from folklore, myth, and astrology. This approach seeks to interpret the symbols of the Apocalypse by comparing them with those found in contemporary culture. Gunkel studied the dragon's battle with the woman and found traces of an oral tradition of a very early origin.

Although the Apocalypse does not contain a single explicit quotation from the Old Testament, nevertheless, it has been estimated that its 404 verses contain about 518 Old Testament allusions and citations. Of these, 88 are from Daniel; about 278 verses are composed of allusions to Ezekiel, Isaiah, Jeremiah, Zechariah, Psalms, and Exodus in addition to Daniel and some of the other Jewish apocalyptic books. The main Jewish Apocalypses are Daniel (167-164 B.C.), Jubilees (150-100 B.C.), Testaments of the Twelve Patriarchs (150-125 B.C.), Assumption of Moses (first century A.D.). 4 Esdras (first century A.D.), 2 Baruch (after A.D. 70), 3 Baruch (2nd century A.D.), and Ethiopian Enoch (ch 1-36 from the second century B.C.; ch 37-71 from the second or third century A.D.).

But John should also be examined against the symbolic world of the people of Asia Minor for whom he wrote. Many tend to recoil today from the extremes of a previous generation of scholars and to insist that the Old Testament provides the basic background. But John and his audience were people who probably knew the folklore and the mythical images of their time. While some rather arbitrary comparisons such as those with the evil Angro-mainyu struggling with the good Ahura-mazda or with the Zoroastrian "folk-angels" can be rejected, one can pursue this rejection too far. The Apocalypse is basically a re-reading of Jewish Apocalyptic in the light of the coming of Jesus of Nazareth. Its purpose is to continue to clarify the history of the people and their struggles with the forces of evil.

7. Liturgical

The whole book is so permeated with liturgical references that several scholars have argued that even in the structure and especially in the frequent hymnic text it follows the liturgy of Asia Minor or a Passover liturgy. This is far from sure. But certain liturgical facts seem evident. The book was intended to be read at a liturgical service (1:3). The beginning and end are framed in a liturgical setting. The key Christian liturgical greeting "grace" is found in 1:4 and repeated in 22:1. The response Amen is continually repeated as the community accepts the statements made in 1:7; 5:14; 7:12; 19:4; 22:20. The earthly liturgical celebration is projected into heaven itself (4:11; 5:9) to bind heaven and earth together in a cosmic celebration. The description of the heavenly Jerusalem is also given a liturgical form (ch 20-21). A comparison with Jewish apocalyptic shows that John has combined another literary form with that of apocalyptic. For the liturgy, particularly the eucharistic liturgy, tends to mould the types of literature which it uses. Thus the Christian liturgy, like apocalyptic literature, speaks of the end but in contrast gives it the name of a person, Jesus. The liturgy is a reminder that Jesus has come and that the hope for the future coming should be joyful and sure.

This liturgical emphasis shows that the Apocalypse is not purely a work of literature. Therefore it can only be properly appreciated in a liturgical atmosphere. According to Paul, apocalypse is a key aspect of the Christian liturgy (1 Cor 14:26). Therefore one can appreciate the suggestion that the best understanding of the Apocalypse is within the liturgy of the Church, particularly the Eucharistic liturgy. For the Eucharist is not only the remembering, the making present of Jesus and his saving work. It also symbolises Jesus' continuing offering of grace to live the Christian life in the present. But especially it offers a foretaste and a pledge of the future glory of the Christian with Christ.

Such an approach counteracts the obsession with history and facts which preoccupies so many Western scholars. No purely scientific examination can reach the basically spiritual message of the Apocalypse. Many Christian communities from El Salvador to Chile, from Zaire to Poland, from Vietnam to Cambodia and Ethiopia, live in a situation very similar to that experienced by John — a repressed minority persecuted often to the point where survival is in jeopardy. The rediscovery of apocalyptic can be seen as one of the signs of our times. John questions us across the centuries particularly in our liturgical assemblies. Is our cry "Come, Lord Jesus!"?

8. *Literary Analysis*

What source material did John use for his work and how did he adapt it? Not unlike the study of the gospels, the literary study of the Apocalypse has proceeded in modern times from Source Criticism through Form Criticism to Redaction Criticism. Particularly in the nineteenth century, the Apocalypse was subjected to a methodic dissection. Many theories of its development were proposed, that it was a document touched up by one or a number of editors, that it was simply the juxtaposition of a number of sources or that it consisted in fragments of older Jewish works. Thus for the German scholar E. Vischer (1886) the main part of the book was a previous Jewish Apocalypse, which was Christianized by the addition of a prologue and an epilogue with a few interpolations added to touch up the main text.

The Irish scholar, R.H. Charles (1855-1931), who was the greatest authority of his time on Jewish eschatology and apocalyptic, and who did so much to restore an appreciation of the true nature of apocalyptic, opened his 1919 lectures on the Apocalypse with the words:

> From the earliest ages of the Church it has been universally admitted that the Apocalypse is the most difficult book of the entire Bible.

In 1921 Charles published the most detailed study hitherto of the Apocalypse in the *International Critical Commentary*. Charles supported the eschatological interpretation. He believed that he could identify the sources, e.g. 7:1-8 coming from a Jewish or Judaeo-Christian source redacted before A.D. 70; 11:1-2 which predicts the preservation of the Temple, coming from a Jewish document before 70; 12:1-5, 13-17 which give a mythic description of Christ, coming from a pagan author. The seven messages were originally seven letters actually sent to the seven churches. When added to the book, the beginnings and endings were adapted to connect them with the rest and their conventional greetings and conclusions were omitted. But they contain conflicting expectations concerning the end of the world. In 2:25 and 3:3 there is the suggestion that the communities will survive until Christ comes. But 3:10 presupposes a world-wide martyrdom. Nevertheless, according to Charles the book has a literary unity and comes from the same author. But John died before completing his work and his disciples' editor, who was "very unintelligent" and "profoundly ignorant of his master's thought," disrupted John's order for the last three chapters.

P. Boismard, who produced the version found in the Jerusalem Bible, believed that John wrote two or more works which ran parallel to each other from chapters 10-21. These were amalgamated, a fact which explains the doublets in the final work. Compare 13:1, 3, 8 with 17:3, 8; 14:8 with 18:2; 12:9, 12 with 20:2-3. Thus he finds duplications of the themes of the beast, the day of wrath, the fall of Babylon, the final battle, and the judgement, and two descriptions of the New Jerusalem in chapters 21-22. In 21:8 (Text II) there is a description of the heavenly Jerusalem, the Church triumphant and glorious when time has passed away. Surprisingly, it is followed by (Text I) the messianic Jerusalem, the Church on earth. The Seer's curse (22:9) prevents him from rearranging these chapters. According to J. Massyngbaerde-Ford, who produced the Anchor Bible volume, chapters 4-11 come from the circle of John the Baptist and pre-date the ministry of Jesus. They are a good description of the Baptist's messianic expectations. Chapters 12-22, dating from the mid 60's, come from disciples of the Baptist and show their expectations with some influence from Christianity. Chapters 1-3 and parts of 22 were added later by a Jewish Christian disciple. However, this theory has not won wide acceptance. The distinctively Christian aspects of chapters 4-11 with their references to the Lamb, his death, and redeeming blood are not easily explained as deriving from the Baptist.

Such minute examinations of a Biblical book tend to leave many people cold. However, they are the basis of almost all recent commentaries and have produced many interesting results, especially a much deeper understanding of this elusive book and its theological message. In general, one can say that there is a reasonable consensus that the Apocalypse as we have it is a theological unity, the careful product of one author. Linguistic studies show that the opening letters are an integral part of the whole. Theological examination shows that it has a genuinely Christian theology if one remembers Raymond Brown's hypothesis (*The Critical Meaning of the Bible*, p 2) that any major book in the Bible taken by itself and pressed on to its logical conclusion can lead to heretical distortions. If one can speak of the assured results of modern critics it is to insist that the Apocalypse must be studied and interpreted as a pastoral book addressed to the historical problems of the Christian communities in Asia Minor. This approach saves the reader from the need to search subsequent history to discover John's characters and their roles. Nevertheless, the Apocalypse is an interpretation of history not only of John's time but of every age.

CONCLUSION

The influence of John's Apocalypse throughout the ages is adequate testimony to the author's creative imagination. However, we need not conclude that his images must be our images. Just as the task for him was to construct a scenario which would help his contemporaries interpret their experience in light of events, so our task is to go and do likewise for our generation.

The mood with which the author leaves us is an overwhelming sense of longing for the fulfilment of what is promised, for the appearance of the one for whom we wait. A story from Ernest Shackleton's exploration of Antarctica illustrates John's point. Once he was compelled to leave most of his band on Elephant Island while with two friends he crossed to South Georgia in an open boat to seek rescuers. Shackleton experienced the mysterious presence of a fourth person with him on his dangerous voyage. But those left behind on Elephant Island waited for days and months for his return. Each day their leader Wild would wake up his companions and encourage them to get on with their work, with the famous words, "Lash up and stow, boys, the boss may come today."

Paul Tillich (*The Shaking of the Foundations*, pp 151f) has some very thought-provoking comments on waiting:

> Both the Old and the New Testaments describe our existence in relation to God as one of waiting . . . . Waiting means not having and having at the same time . . . . The condition of man's relation to God is first of all one of not having, not seeing, not knowing, and not grasping . . . . I think of the theologian who does not wait for God, because he possesses him enclosed within a doctrine. I think of the biblical student who does not wait for God, because he possesses him enclosed in a book. I think of the churchman who does not wait for God, because he possesses him enclosed in an institution. I think of the believer who does not wait for God, because he possesses him enclosed within his own experience. It is not easy to endure this, not having God, this waiting for God. It is not easy to preach Sunday after Sunday without convincing ourselves and others that we have God and can dispose of him. It is not easy to proclaim God to children and pagans, to sceptics and secularists, and at the same time to make clear to them that we ourselves do not possess God, that we too wait for him. I am convinced that much of the rebellion against Christianity, is due to the overt or veiled claim of the Christians to possess God, and therefore, also, to the loss of this element of waiting, so decisive for the prophets and the apostles . . . They did not possess God; they waited for him. For how can God be possessed? Is God a thing that can be grasped and known among other things? Is God less than a human person? We always have to wait for a human

being. Even in the most intimate communion among human beings, there is an element of not having and not knowing, and of waiting. Therefore, since God is infinitely hidden, free and incalculable,we must wait for him in the most absolute and radical way. He is God for us just in so far as we do not possess him ... We have God through not having him.

FURTHER READING

Ashcroft, M., *Revelation*, The Broadman Bible Commentary, (Broadman, Nashville, 1972).

Barclay, W., *The Revelation*, (Saint Andrew, Edinburgh, 1976; Westminster, Philadelphia, 1976).

Brown, R. E., S. S., *The Critical Meaning of the Bible*, (Paulist, New York, 1981).

Caird, G. B., *The Revelation of St. John the Divine*, (Harper & Row, New York, 1966).

Collins, A. Yarbro, *The Apocalypse*, (Michael Glazier, Inc., Wilmington, 1979).

―――――――― *Crisis and Catharsis*, (Westminster, Philadelphia, 1984).

Court, J. M., *Myth and History in the Book of Revelation*, (John Knox, Atlanta, 1979).

Feuillet, A., *The Apocalypse*, (Alba House, New York, 1965).

Glasson, T. F., *The Revelation of John*, (Cambridge U., Cambridge, 1965).

Hanson, P. D., (ed), *Visionaries and Their Apocalypses*, (SPCK, London, 1983; Fortress, Philadelphia, 1983).

Harrington, W., O. P., *Understanding the Apocalypse*, (Corpus, Washington, 1969).

Johnson, A. F., *Revelation*, The Expositor's Bible Commentary, (Eerdmans, Grand Rapids, 1981).

Massyngbaerde-Ford, J., *Revelation*, (Doubleday, New York, 1975).

McGinn, B. (Introduction and Translation), *Apocalyptic Spirituality*, (Paulist, New York, 1979).

Minear, S., *I Saw a New Earth*, (Corpus, Washington, 1968)

——————— *New Testament Apocalyptic*, (Abingdon, Nashville, 1981).

Morris, L., *Revelation*, (Inter Varsity, Leicester, 1983; Eerdmans, Grand Rapids, 1983).

Pedersen, J., *Israel*, (Oxford University, New York, 1926, 1948).

Schillebeeckx, E., *Jesus*, (Collins, London, 1979; Seabury, New York, 1979).

Schüssler-Fiorenza, E., *Invitation to the Book of Revelation*, (Doubleday, New York, 1981).

Sena, P. J., C.P.P.S., *The Apocalypse*, (Alba House, New York, 1983).

Stringfellow, W., *An Ethic For Christians and Other Aliens in a Strange Land*, (Word, Waco, Texas, 1973).

Sweet, J. P. M., *Revelation*, (Westminster, Philadelphia, 1979).

NAME INDEX

SUBJECT INDEX

Amen 71, 104

Angels 86, 99. 145-146, 153, 154-156, 169-170, 182, 184-188, 190, 192, 194-195, 228

Anger of God (See Wrath of God)

Antichrist, the 174, 177-178, 180, 240-241, 242

Apocalypse, the
— arts and 23-26, 107, 110, 111, 162-163, 164, 210, 221
— as catharsis 31-32
— as counterculture 29-30
— as history 242-244
— as prophecy 45, 48, 49, 50-53, 64, 239-241
— authorship of 55-60, 232
— canonicity of 20-21
— Christology of 38-40, 68-69, 74-77, 104, 126, 130, 136, 214-215
— God in 36-37, 65, 67-70
— imagination and 33-36, 51, 53
— literary criticism and 247-250

— liturgy and 74, 118-127, 145-146, 163-164, 209-213, 245-246
— morality and 42-44, 82
— Old Testament and 52, 55, 65, 70, 72, 82, 128-129, 155, 245-246
— Rome and 30, 44-45, 47, 49, 54, 57-60, 66, 71, 85-86, 88, 89, 118, 130-131, 133, 172-181, 193, 199, 201-209, 242-244
— Spirit in 40-41, 68, 74, 84
— symbolism, use of, in 53-55, 64, 114-115, 202
— theological controversy and 20-23, 30-31

Apocalyptic, apocalypticism 11-16, 18-23, 26, 30-31, 48-53, 64, 236

Babylon 45, 185-186, 187, 196, 199, 200-209

Beast from the Land 177-181

Beast from the Sea 160, 172-177

Blessing (meaning of) 63, 232-233

Book of Life 221